The Teaching Church at Work

A Manual for the Board of Christian Education

Revised Edition

Kenneth D. Blazier and Linda R. Isham, Editors

Judson Press ® Valley Forge

The Teaching Church at Work: A Manual for the Board of Christian Education
Revised Edition

© 1993
Judson Press, Valley Forge, PA 19482-0851

Library of Congress Cataloging-in-Publication Data

The teaching church at work : a manual for the board of Christian
  education / edited by Kenneth D. Blazier and Linda R. Isham. — Rev.
ed.
      p.   cm.
    Includes bibliographical references.
    ISBN 0-8170-1191-9
    1. Christian education—Handbooks, manuals, etc. I. Blazier,
Kenneth D. II. Isham, Linda R.
  BV1471.2.T44   1993
  268′.1—dc20   93-31239

Printed in the U.S.A.

      97 98 99 00 01 02
  9 8 7 6 5 4 3

Contents

To our mentor and friend,
Kenneth L. Cober

Preface

This manual has been written for the group that is responsible for a church's ministry and program of Christian education. At the heart of its content is the concept or understanding of a local church as a "teaching (and learning) church."

The purpose of this manual is to help the board or committee of Christian education (or group assigned to the task) become more effective in planning and implementing the total program of Christian education within the church. An overview and practical how-to suggestions are given in relationship to several aspects of the total work of the board.

Although the manual may be helpful when it is read from cover to cover, especially by a new member of the board, its primary value will probably be realized when a board member turns to a given chapter as help is sought in relation to some specific aspect of the responsibility of the board.

The manual is in three parts. Part I, "Understanding the Task," interprets the concept of a "teaching church" (chapter 1), suggests ways a board may review the goal of the church's teaching ministry (chapter 2), determines the purpose of its teaching ministry (chapter 3), and explores learning in a teaching church (chapter 4).

In Part II, "Organizing the Board," specific helps are provided in relation to the functions (chapter 5) and organization or structure of the board (chapter 6), job descriptions for workers (chapter 7), and the life of the board as a group (chapter 8).

Part III, "Developing the Program," presents basic information and helps for the board as it plans the total educational program. As background, it considers the characteristics and needs of persons at various points in their life cycle (chapter 9) and in chapter 10 gives an overview of teaching-learning programs (programs of ongoing nurture, programs in response to teachable moments, and programs built around the church year). Chapter 11 outlines a leadership development plan. Chapter 12 outlines an evaluation-planning process for the board using nine characteristics of effective and vital Christian education. The final chapter encourages the board in the essential task of developing congregational support for the teaching ministry (chapter 13).

This manual is a revision of *The Teaching Church at Work* edited by Kenneth D. Blazier. While this revised edition includes two additional chapters (chapters 4 and 11) and a replacement chapter (12), most of the changes have been of an updating nature. It has been a joy to work with and build upon such a solid foundation. I am grateful to Ken for his earlier work and to our mentor Kenneth L. Cober whose book *Shaping the Church's Educational Ministry* forms the footings for this as well as the earlier edition.

The material in this manual was written by Christian education colleagues of mine. Grant W. Hanson, retired Director of the Division of Church Education of Educational Ministries, wrote chapters 1, 2, and 3. Marsha McDaniel, Minister of Education, First Baptist Church, Indianapolis, Indiana, wrote chapter 4. Co-editor Kenneth Blazier wrote chapters 5, 6, and 7. Vergie Gillespie, retired program director, Educational Ministries, wrote chapters 8 and 13. Joe H. Leonard, Jr., family life consultant in Wayne, Pennsylvania, wrote chapters 9 and 10. John L. "Bud" Carroll, Deputy Director for Regional Relations, Educational Ministries, wrote chapter 11. I wrote chapter 12 and edited this revision.

It is the hope and prayer of the writers and editors that this manual will provide practical help and encouragement for persons responsible for planning effective and vital Christian education. Nothing matters more in the development of faithful mature Christians and congregations than effective Christian education!

—Linda R. Isham

Chapter 1

Understanding the Concept of a "Teaching Church"

There are many ways of viewing the church as is clear from the variety of word images found in the New Testament. It is important to remember that no single way of talking about the church is ever totally adequate to communicate the fullness of its nature and mission. However we describe it, the church is always that and something more.

Many Christians have found it extremely helpful to think of the church as a teaching community. As such, it is a community of persons, drawn together by their commitment to Jesus Christ, who develop and extend that community through the ministry of teaching. It is necessary, of course, that teaching be understood in the most inclusive terms and not in a narrow or restricted sense.

This manual is based on the premise that the educational task of the church is best understood by beginning with the concept of a "teaching church." We move now to the development of that concept.

Affirmations about a "Teaching Church"

A teaching church models the ministry of its Lord

In its teaching ministry the church is most like the Master whom it serves. People called Jesus many things during the years of his ministry, but the most common term was *teacher*. In his relationship with the group of disciples closest to him he was first and foremost the teacher. It is fair to say that basically his was a ministry of teaching.

When Jesus gave his charge to the first-century church, he said, "Go therefore and make disciples of all nations, . . . teaching them . . ." (Matthew 28:19–20). These familiar words, which we know as the Great Commission, are frequently related to the imperative for evangelism. They are certainly no less an imperative for Christian teaching. The word *disciple* is to be interpreted *learner* or *pupil*. The command is literally to "make pupils" ("teaching them"). The words could not be more explicit.

A teaching church unifies a variety of ministries

In his book, *The Church's Teaching Ministry*, Kenneth Cober identifies six functions or ministries within the whole ministry of the church: proclamation, teaching, worship, fellowship, witness, and service. He points out that the relationship of Christian education to these other ministries has not always been recognized.[1] There is a very primary relationship in which the teaching ministry undergirds and supports the other ministries.

Proclamation is at the heart of the gospel. The Good News exists to be shared. Persons need help in learning how to express that Good News so that they may share in proclamation.

Participation in **worship** requires growing understanding and experience. Persons need to be introduced to the heritage and resources of worship and then taught how to practice the related disciplines of Bible reading and prayer.

Fellowship must be experienced to be understood. As a teaching community, the church offers many group experiences in which persons discover the meaning of Christian fellowship.

Witness occurs when persons have been trained and motivated to share their faith. The purpose of the teaching ministry is to teach persons to incorporate the truth of Christ in their lives in ways that make it possible to communicate both verbally and nonverbally. In proclamation the emphasis is on the message and the act of proclaiming; in witness the Christian is interpreting a personal and deep experience.

An effective teaching ministry is directed outward to the world where the ministry of **service** is needed. The link is established between the church as servant and the arenas of human need that call for help.

A teaching church witnesses in word and deed

There is an old saying: "Do not do as I do; do as I say." By contrast Jesus said, ". . . let your light shine before others, so that they may see your good works . . ." (Matthew 5:16). To keep teaching and example consistent is an age-old problem.

A teaching church knows that everything depends on the quality of life that it evidences. The Christian faith is perhaps more an experience of contagion than instruction. Persons are loved, not argued, into the kingdom. When this quality of life is missing, the church is basically ineffective.

The community of faith at its best teaches volumes by the quality of its life together. Unplanned learning is as real as the most carefully planned learning. Education is informal as well as formal.

A church is constantly teaching in all that it does, in the ways it thinks, in the attitudes it evidences, in its treatment of persons, and in the values that it makes primary. Teaching is not a special type of activity restricted to limited, formal situations. Teaching is the whole life of this special community that we call the church. When the church is described as the body of Christ, the focus is upon Christ's living presence in the world

---

[1] Kenneth L. Cober, *The Church's Teaching Ministry*. (Valley Forge: Judson Press, 1964), 34–36.

involved in ministry. A teaching church is called to be the living embodiment of the One who came that all might have life, and that more abundantly.

Functions of a Teaching Church

When a church begins to think of itself as a teaching church, it has an organizing principle around which it can build its educational ministry. There are at least five basic functions that must be carried out if a church is to fulfill its teaching ministry.

Function: To affirm the foundations of its teaching ministry

A teaching church begins with the biblical revelation and the Christian heritage. As it assimilates these biblical, theological, and historical perspectives, its teaching is made relevant and significant when it brings the light of the gospel to bear upon the life issues of today. Without adequate biblical and theological rootage the teaching ministry can never fulfill its basic commission. The safeguard against perversion of error is an adequate grounding in the tenets of the historic faith.

An understanding and appreciation of the continuing work of the Holy Spirit in the ministry of teaching are necessary parts of the foundation. Christian teaching is always more than a human enterprise. It is a sacred responsibility that has about it a dimension of mystery and wonder.

The foundations of the teaching ministry also include an understanding of the nature of growing persons. Effective teaching always takes into account the persons who are being taught. An awareness of the many ways persons grow sharpens sensitivity to the uniqueness of every human being.

The learning process itself is also an important aspect of the foundation for teaching. To understand how persons learn is basic to meaningful teaching ministry.

Function: To plan for the most effective teaching ministry

Planning is key to an effective teaching ministry. A teaching church establishes its goals and then plans for their accomplishment. Goals that are significant emerge out of the awareness of the needs of persons in the light of the gospel. Each church accepts the responsibility for defining its specific goals based on the perceptions of its particular situation.

Organizational structures are necessary to carry the responsibility for planning and administering a program. A duly constituted board or committee charged with overseeing the total educational program (called a board of Christian education in this manual) will tend to foster coordination and comprehensiveness. This manual is intended to be a basic tool in assisting the board or committee to discover and carry out its responsibility. In situations where there is no board or committee and an individual or informal group of individuals carries the responsibilities this book can be a helpful tool as well.

An essential element in successful program development is the involvement and support of the congregation. A teaching church cannot fulfill its ministry unless the whole congregation is involved. Good planning makes provision for giving the congregation a sense of "ownership." Without ownership the level of commitment on the part of members is minimal.

Function: To develop leaders for a variety of ministries

A teaching church cannot function without a corps of leaders prepared to fulfill a variety of ministries. These leaders must be recruited, motivated, trained, assigned, and supported. Their development includes personal growth, understanding of the learning processes, sensitivity to the needs of persons, and acquisition of basic skills. The quality of the program is largely dependent on the quality of leadership. Because the need for new leaders is constant, the plan of enlistment, training, and support must be ongoing.

A teaching church is concerned, furthermore, not simply about the designated leaders but about the broader responsibility of "equipping persons for ministry." Everyone in the community of faith has gifts, recognized or unrecognized. If the gifts are unrecognized, they need to be discovered. An aspect of the Christian growth of every person is the development of the capacity to exercise leadership in one form or another.

Function: To nurture persons in Christian growth

A teaching church is a nurturing community. Its goal is to provide a loving, caring environment in which persons can grow in the Christian faith and experience. It recognizes that the Christian life is a maturing process with many stages of development from infancy to adulthood. Persons within a single congregation reflect many degrees of progress toward the objective of maturity. There is a beautiful blend of naiveté and sophistication, ignorance and wisdom, inexperience and experience. All are learners, and all are teachers. The interaction and interrelationship across the total life cycle enrich the experience of all.

Growing persons are helped most when there has been intentional planning. It is important that the church set out deliberately to provide learning experiences for persons of all ages, in which they can come to understand themselves and their experiences in the light of the gospel. A church needs to design an educational program that in systematic fashion seeks to support the growth process.

The quality of life of the congregation is a vital factor in effective nurture. Much learning is unplanned and unintentional. When there is inconsistency between what the congregation professes and what it practices, negative learning is a real possibility. A teaching church needs to remember that it is called above all else to be a redemptive community that gives and supports life.

Function: To support the fulfillment of the church's mission in the world

A teaching church recognizes that it always exists in relation to the world. Its ministry attempts to bridge the gospel and the world. It is concerned with fostering the intersection of the Christian faith with life.

A part of growing as an individual Christian is the development of a sense of vocation. Involvement in mission is the normal expectation for all who seek to live as disciples of Jesus Christ.

It is important, moreover, that a teaching church express its involvement in mission corporately. God's calling is to the church collectively as well as individually. The church involved in a community ministry is fulfilling its teaching role in a most telling way.

Together, these five functions provide a conceptual framework upon which a church can build its ministry of teaching. They help to answer the question about the scope of the task faced by a church that wants to take its responsibility seriously.

Learning in a Teaching Church

A teaching church is also always a learning church. Learning is a part of the stance taken by a teaching church. The Bible calls us to such an understanding. Isaiah 50:4 and Matthew 11:28–29 are examples of that call.

Learning is a lifelong pursuit for the individual Christian and for a Christian community. God, through Jesus Christ, calls us into an ongoing learning relationship. We are learners in relationship to God and are called to be learners in relation to others and the world as well.

Often, unless we draw special attention to learning in relation to teaching, learning is overlooked. So we need to address learning specifically within the context of a teaching church. Chapter 4 in this manual addresses this issue.

Chapter 2

Reviewing the Goal of the Church's Teaching Ministry

The goal of the church's educational ministry is that all persons be aware of God through God's self-disclosure, especially God's redeeming love as revealed in Jesus Christ, and, enabled by the Holy Spirit, respond in faith and love; that they may become new persons in Christ, know who they are and what their human situation means, grow as children of God rooted in the Christian community, live in obedience to the will of God in every relationship, fulfill their common vocation in the world, and abide in Christian hope.

A second way of understanding the educational task of the church is to focus on a goal or hoped-for outcome. Instead of thinking in terms of functions, leaders should direct attention toward a goal to be accomplished and view the task from the perspective of the target toward which they are aiming. A goal has several purposes:

- It helps leaders to determine the form and content of the teaching program;
- It provides leaders with a sense of direction and a means of charting progress;
- It offers a framework for evaluating the achievements of the overall teaching program.

In 1965 sixteen Protestant denominations, working together in the Cooperative Curriculum Project, adopted a statement of the "Objective of the Church's Educational Ministry." The statement describes the overall goal for a church's teaching program. Using that statement as a basis, various groups have developed their own statements. One of those statements is printed at the beginning of this chapter. The following is an interpretation of that statement:

The goal of the church's educational ministry is

An effective teaching ministry is built upon the common understanding by a congregation of its objective. There are basic questions that must be answered, such as "What do we want to see happen in the educational program?" "What is the ultimate goal?" "How do we know that we have achieved it?"

that all persons

The church's teaching ministry must have the same universality as does the gospel. It is inclusive. There are no barriers. It is never intended just for those presently within

the Christian fellowship. The Good News is for everyone, and to make it provincial is
heresy.

be aware of God

The experience of the reality of God in personal terms is the heart of the teaching
ministry. God is not a subject to be studied. Awareness cuts to the innermost core of
being. God is to be known and experienced at the very center of life as the ultimate of
all realities.

through God's self-disclosure,

God is known because God has chosen to be revealed through creation in the lives of
individuals of faith, in life in the world, and supremely in the person of Jesus Christ.
The record of this revelation has been preserved in the Scriptures. The church regards
the Bible as the normative means by which God's word comes to us.

especially God's redeeming love as revealed in Jesus Christ,

The faith of the church is centered upon the figure of Jesus Christ who is the supreme
revelation of God's love for the world. In the person of this one who comes to identify
fully with humanity the divine love reaches out to reconcile all unto itself. The life,
death, and resurrection of Jesus are God's message to all who have been alienated
that their bondage has been broken and that they have new life and a new relationship with God and one another.

and, enabled by the Holy Spirit,

God's continuing activity in the lives of individuals makes possible their response.
The initiative and the empowerment are of God. The church's teaching ministry is
made effective because God is at work in it through the Spirit's continuing presence
in the world.

respond in faith and love,

God is always reaching out, but at some moment there must be a response to that
redeeming love. The act of faith is to accept what has been offered and to love as one
has first been loved by God. The response is voluntary. The freedom of the will is
inviolate. Persons choose whether to respond.

that they may become new persons in Christ,

The result of the response of faith is the creation of a new person. The change is so
total that the only adequate description of the new life lived in Christ is a "new person." This transforming experience is a basic concern of the teaching ministry. Teaching is to the end that persons be changed and live henceforth to manifest a newness
of life.

know who they are and what their human situation means,

Life is filled with many questions that demand answers. Basic are the questions about
the nature, the purpose, the meaning, and the ultimate destiny of life. Without answers to these questions it is impossible to establish values, to set goals, or to find
meanings. The Christian faith addresses itself to just such persistent life issues.

grow as children of God

Growth is natural for all living things. Growth for the Christian is relational. It is
toward God. It is toward other persons. The objective of growth is maturity. In the
words of the writer of Ephesians the goal is "the measure of the full stature of Christ"
(Ephesians 4:13). While attainment is never complete, there is movement toward that
ultimate ideal and a sense of growing fulfillment.

rooted in the Christian community,

The roots for Christian growth are found in the community of faith. The community provides the atmosphere of love and concern in which growth can flourish. To attempt to live apart from that nurturing context is to court disaster. Within the community the Christian learns the meaning of the servant role and finds his or her place of ministry. All that the community is and does contributes to the total educational process.

live in obedience to the will of God in every relationship,

The sign of the new life in Christ is obedience to the will of God in every aspect of life. The concept of Christ's lordship brings all of life under his dominion. Life cannot be compartmentalized but must always be dealt with holistically. The solid evidence of the new life is the demonstration that all actions and all relationships are consistent with the will of God.

fulfill their common vocation in the world,

Christians have a common vocation, which is the ministry of reconciliation. The arena for that ministry is the whole world. Wherever there is brokenness, hostility, estrangement, or alienation, the Christian is called to be healer, peacemaker, and reconciler. This was the ministry Christ came to perform and which is given now to his followers. The church must prepare and equip its members for this calling.

and abide in the Christian hope.

There is much of life that is uncertain and unpredictable. It has its high moments and its low moments. There is a constancy for the Christian, however, found in the hope rooted in the eternal God who is above and beyond all limits of time and space. The Christian faces the future in faith, knowing that the last word will be God's. This hope brings a perspective by which to understand the past, rise to the challenge of the present, and have confidence about the future.

Chapter 3

Determining the Purpose of the Church's Teaching Ministry

A third way of better understanding the educational task of the church is to engage in a process of determining the purpose for your church's teaching ministry. If a church has never specifically done this, there is probably an untested assumption that everyone understands what that purpose is. However, a uniform understanding is seldom true.

A good statement of purpose communicates very clearly what a church sees as its task. It provides a common frame of reference in which all educational leaders can work together. If the statement is to have these characteristics, it needs to be the product of a group endeavor in which all persons have an investment and for which they have a sense of ownership. The workshop design that follows is intended to assist a group of leaders to develop a statement of purpose for Christian education in their church.

Workshop on a Church's Purpose of Christian Education

Objective: To formulate a workable statement of purpose for Christian education in our church.

Participants: Board of Christian education, church school teachers and officers, age-group leaders, pastor(s), church officers, and other concerned persons.

Time: Two hours.

Supplies: Paper and pencils, Bibles, newsprint, and felt-tip pens or crayons.

Plan for the workshop:

Step 1: *Look at our current Christian education program* in light of the five functions of the teaching church in chapter 1 (15 minutes).

- Around the room post five sheets of newsprint with one of the five functions listed at the top of each, as follows:

to affirm the foundations of its teaching ministry

to plan for the most effective teaching ministry

to develop leaders for a variety of ministries

to nurture persons in Christian growth

to enable the fulfillment of the church's mission in the world

Leave lots of space below the headings on each sheet.

- As the group assembles, encourage persons to go in pairs to the newsprint and record the thoughts that come to them on the respective sheets as they answer the question, "What does each statement suggest to us about what we are doing or ought to be doing in our teaching ministry?" The task is to generate as many thoughts and ideas as possible.
- When the work on the newsprint is complete, ask the pairs to come together as a total group to reflect on the items recorded on the various sheets. Invite them to discuss what has been said about the church's program of Christian education. Questions for discussion may include:

How do we as Christian education leaders perceive our teaching program?

In what ways might our perception differ from those of other persons in the church?

What are some of the ways in which our church could be helped to have a clearer understanding of the purpose of its teaching ministry?

Step 2: *Examine a biblical perspective on the teaching ministry* (20 minutes).

- In groups of three read and discuss Ephesians 4:1-16. The assignment is to discover what the passage says about the teaching ministry of the church. Questions for discussion may include:

What comprises the "life worthy of the calling"?

How is a sense of unity and oneness fostered in a church?

In what ways are persons helped to discover and develop their gifts?

- Share together in the total group the insights from the biblical reflection.
- Have the group members summarize on newsprint what they feel are the most significant insights from the biblical material. Underline phrases that are particularly helpful.

Step 3: *Consider the values of developing a statement of purpose* (10 minutes).

- Put on newsprint the following values of a purpose statement:

A statement of purpose for Christian education will give us:

1. a check on the various perceptions of our purpose as held by members of the congregation,
2. a basic statement of what the church sees as our teaching task,
3. a common goal for all planning and program development,
4. a clearer understanding among the leaders about what they are asked to do,
5. a frame of reference for program evaluation,
6. an opportunity for ownership by the congregation of the teaching task.

- The group members can discuss these statements and add others that they feel are appropriate.
- At the conclusion there should be consensus that a good statement of purpose will contribute to a more effective teaching ministry.

Step 4: *Develop the first draft of a statement of purpose* (50 minutes).

- Ask everyone to reflect for a few minutes and write down what he or she feels is the primary task of Christian education in the church. This question might be posed: "What are we in business to do educationally?" Allow not more than five minutes for the assignment.

- Share the responses in the total group, pausing for clarification or questions. Ask the group members to note when they hear a key concept or a meaningful phrase in the course of the discussion. Record these on newsprint for future reference.

- After everyone has shared his or her response, have the group look at the key concepts or meaningful phrases charted on the newsprint. Ask each person to choose three to five (depending on your group size) that they feel are most important to include in a statement of purpose. Record these choices on the newsprint, tallying the votes and noting which items have the most votes.

- Divide into groups of three with the assignment to develop a one-sentence statement based upon the three to five most important items checked on the newsprint: "The purpose of Christian education in our church is. . . ." Have the groups put their statements on newsprint. Allow fifteen minutes for the assignment.

- Have the statements read aloud and posted for the total group. Lead the group in reaching consensus on the one statement that is the most meaningful and helpful. Encourage the group to discuss it.

- Test to see if the statement is one that all people present are ready to support. If it is, proceed to step 5. If not, work on refining it until there is a consensus that the statement is acceptable.

Step 5: *Plan the next steps for the adoption of the statement* (15 minutes).

- Determine how the statement can be shared with the official boards and the membership at large and what procedure there should be for recording suggestions or reactions.

- Agree on a revision procedure and assign the responsibility.

- Propose a plan for official action by the board of Christian education and the congregation when the statement is in final form.

- Develop a list of suggestions for publicizing the statement and helping the congregation to be aware of it.

- Set a time for review of the statement and its possible revision.

Step 6: *Reflect upon the meaning of the workshop experience* (10 minutes).

- Share personal feelings about the experience of considering the purpose of Christian education. Highlight any learning or insights that may have come.

- Spend the closing moments in prayer.

Chapter 4

Exploring Learning in a Teaching Church

The teaching church is also a learning church. It is a church faithfully participating in the ongoing process of understanding and changing the world; of fostering a responsible, loving relationship with God, with humankind, and all creation; and of equipping its people for ministry. Learning is the basis for our role as teachers. What we have seen and heard as learners helps us serve as teachers with others. (See 2 Timothy 2:2; Proverbs 1:2-7; 3:5-6; Deuteronomy 4:9-10.)

It is through learning that we begin to understand who we are and whose we are, that we can find purpose and meaning for life and discover solutions to problems we encounter. Learning can provide a means for coping with changes in our life situations, such as death, chronic illness, parenthood, retirement, divorce, job change or loss, conflict. These changes, in turn, can create new questions and challenges for us. Learning can provide a bridge of understanding between cultures and races, traditions and perspectives.

If we are to be faithful to our educational task, we must recognize individual and corporate learning as a vital part of that task. The message we proclaim, our relationship with God and other persons, our witness in word and deed, and the Christian service we extend are all influenced by our learning. The future and ministry of the church depends upon our readiness and dedication to be a teaching-learning church.

What is learning? How is it related to teaching?

Historically there are two basic theories about learning: the behavioral or "spectator" theory and the cognitive or "participant" theory. Students and followers of each theory have written much in the way of explanation. The differences in the theories lie primarily in two areas: how learning occurs and the role of the learner. In each theory the concept of learning controls the concept of teaching. It may be helpful as you read about these two basic theories to read with the eyes and mind of a learner.

According to the behavioral theory, learning occurs as a physical response to stimuli outside the learner; thus, learning is basically a change in behavior. Although the learner is rewarded for a desired behavior, the learner is more or less passive in the process. Hence, this is sometimes called the "spectator" theory. Teaching is mostly a matter of telling and reinforcing what is told. Learning or change is imposed from outside the learner and generally is seen to be controlled by the teacher. We are familiar with this theory of learning through computer-assisted instruction and behavior modification techniques. It is a theory often used by parents of young children who want to modify certain behaviors such as running into the street and by adults who are on a controlled diet plan.

According to the cognitive theory, learning is a mental reorganization of the environment through experience and insight. Learners are actively involved in the process as they select, reduce, elaborate, transform, store, and use data from the environment. Hence, this is also referred to as the "participant" theory. Learning or change occurs as experiences and thoughts are shaped and influenced through the process of reorganization. Teaching is a matter of structuring the learning event so that specified, desired outcomes for the learner are the result. We are familiar with this learning theory through workshops, discussion groups, and learning centers. It is a theory used by preschool teachers in learning centers and by adults and youth involved in independent study.

Over the years students of learning have come to realize that each theory, although having a different approach, has something to offer to our understanding of learning. From the behavioral theory we realize that learning involves change in behavior and needs to be supported or reinforced. From the cognitive theory we realize that learning requires the active involvement of the learner and needs to begin at a point that is meaningful for the learner. From studying both theories we realize that learning is a complex endeavor that engages the whole person—mind, body, and emotions.

In a teaching church, as described in this book, the learning approach is more compatible with, but not limited to, the cognitive theory of learning. In a teaching church, then, learning is a process of taking in information and incorporating it into one's life, of making meaning and connections, and of reconstructing one's view of the world, of self, of God, and of Jesus Christ. Learning is active and intentional. It implies change in one's knowing, feeling, and doing and it may mean reordering one's life. It involves becoming aware, discerning what is true or reliable, and expanding one's understanding. Learning is not for timid souls, because it is a high risk venture, requiring those who participate in it to loosen their grip on what is known, to look again, to test and possibly assimilate what is new. For some persons learning may be a painful process because it may mean giving up old ways of thinking and old ways of doing things. For some persons learning may be ". . . like gentle rain on grass, like showers on new growth" (Deuteronomy 32:2) because it may mean new insights or solutions to problems.

In a teaching church, learning includes, but is more than, listening to a lecture or filling in the blanks on a worksheet or painting a picture. It is more than memorizing the names of the twelve disciples or repeating what is written in the study guide or changing bad habits. Learning involves our minds and our hearts, our feelings and our thoughts, our wills and our actions. Learning involves growth that begins in the earliest days of life and continues for as long as we live. We are all responsible for our own learning. We can learn with and from others, but we cannot depend upon someone else to learn for us.

Unfortunately, within our society learning has become synonymous with schooling, which is generally associated with younger, less experienced, or less knowledgeable persons. The teaching-learning church knows this is not true. Wherever faithful disciples of Jesus Christ gather, everyone is a learner whether young or old, experienced or inexperienced, knowledgeable or uninformed. Learning spans the ages. The teaching-learning church recognizes learning as a process whereby God "will write it on their hearts; . . . from the least of them to the greatest" (Jeremiah 31:33-34).

While learning is ultimately the responsibility of the individual, it is assisted by other persons. Another way to state this idea is that teachers guide the learning process by arranging the conditions for learning. Teachers furnish and organize information, locate resources, ask questions and actively listen, demonstrate skills, help to clarify problems, provide encouragement. Teachers in the church also share their faith journeys with students and challenge students to faithful discipleship. Whatever teachers do in a learning situation, they are, in reality, servants of learning, ministering to the learners. In some ways teaching is like being a midwife (one who gives assistance in bringing forth something new), or to use Paul's metaphor in 1 Corinthians 3:6, teaching is like being a gardener (one who plants and waters the seed) with God causing the growth.

The role of teacher is not one to be taken lightly for it is a role of great responsibility. Check the warnings in Matthew 5:19; Romans 2:17-23; Titus 2:7; James 3. Teachers are to be persons of integrity, knowledge, and understanding; for they, along with prophets, evangelists, and pastors, have been given the responsibility of building up the body of Christ (Ephesians 4:11-13). The role of teacher is, indeed, a role of sacred trust. However, it is not a task one fulfills alone. God is always present in the teaching-learning process. Although teachers may be responsible for initiating and facilitating the learning process, they are also learners. Persons who serve in a teaching role for any length of time are very much aware of this fact. They know that to teach is to learn. Many times teachers are heard to say that they have learned more than their students.

The relationship of teacher and learner is not one of a superior to an inferior person, but rather the relationship is one of a guide and/or mentor to other persons who share the journey. Teaching and learning are two parts of a whole, where "those who are taught" share what they learn with their teachers (Galatians 6:6). It is a process somewhat like riding a seesaw with a rhythm of giving and receiving. Teachers and learners, regardless of age or background, can share knowledge and experience with each other that can benefit everyone.

How Does Learning Happen?

There are many avenues for learning. Persons can learn while alone, with a partner, or in groups. They can learn in formal or informal settings, through drama or service projects, reading or listening. The combinations of setting, activity, and learner are limited only by the imagination of the persons responsible for planning teaching-learning events. The creativity and possibilities for learning can be exciting and fun, but they must always take into consideration two basic elements: (a) the receptivity or readiness of the learner and (b) the appropriateness of the method for the learner. If either of these elements is ignored, learning can be difficult and unpleasant at best or misguided at worst. Or learning may not happen at all.

Learning happens in what has been called "teachable moments," when learners are open to new ideas or experiences and the possibility of change. Some teachable moments may be the result of transitions in life or personal crisis, questions or feelings of inadequacy; at other times these moments may be based on curiosity, internal conflict, personal goals, or a search for meaning.

Learners respond best when the activities and methods are appropriate for the learners' abilities and preferences. For example, young children think in concrete terms and have very little sense of history. They will not understand, nor likely care, that Moses lived before Jesus, but young children can understand that Moses and Jesus were people who grew up and helped other people. Children can enjoy dressing in biblical costumes or singing a lullaby or helping a friend as they learn about Moses and Jesus. Teachers who work with young children realize that their task is more a task of introducing biblical persons and events to the children than it is giving a full and detailed explanation.

Although older children continue to think in concrete terms, they are developing skills in reading and writing and can begin to put things in categories and sequences. They may enjoy retelling Bible stories through cartoon-style drawings or playing games designed to help them remember the books of the Bible or writing a play about Jesus going to Jerusalem with his parents. Teachers who work with older children recognize their task as one of introducing the biblical story and building on what is already known.

As persons reach adolescence, the capacity to reason and think more abstractly grows stronger. This capacity allows for activities such as discussion about the nature of the church, reflection on one's faith journey, and interpretation of biblical passages. This capacity also allows for persons to imagine what it might have been like to be in a storm-tossed boat and see Jesus walking toward them or to be a friend of Lydia's and to have watched how she changed. Teachers working with adolescents realize that their task includes inviting persons to risk exploring how the biblical message can be incorporated into their lives and how they will respond faithfully as disciples of Jesus Christ.

Adults have the capacity to reason and think abstractly about matters of faith. Many adults are seeking to put together an integrated, mature Christian faith. They will respond best when the content and method relate to their needs, gifts, and life experience. In-depth Bible study, discussion, role play, and case studies are all appropriate methods to be used with adults. Teachers of adults recognize their task as one of challenging students to be open to lifelong learning and to faithful discipleship.

As these examples indicate, there is an expansion in the repertoire of ways learning occurs as persons move from childhood through adolescence and adulthood. There is one constant in every learning situation, however, and that is the need to begin at a meaningful point for the learners. This means that whatever is being taught needs to be related in a meaningful way to what is already known.

Another way to describe how learning happens is to consider individual learning styles or, in other words, how a person (of any age) prefers to take in information in order to make sense of it. Some persons prefer seeing. These learners may enjoy reading, movies, bulletin board displays, art, pictures, maps, charts, nature objects, and demonstrations. Some persons prefer hearing. These learners may enjoy books on tape, reader's theater, lectures, hearing the Bible read aloud, recordings, music, stories, and discussion. Some persons prefer touching and moving. These learners may enjoy painting murals, acting out stories, taking field trips, writing a litany, games, role play, using rhythm instruments, and making puppets. It may come as no surprise that many persons prefer a combination of learning styles. These learners, and, in fact, learners of any style, may enjoy learning centers where there are several opportunities to experience, to hear and see, and where they may choose activities that interest them most. Learning centers also provide opportunity for the learner to expand his or her learning style preferences.

The most effective learning situations will offer a variety of learning activities so that each learner will benefit. When learning styles are taken into consideration, the underlying message is that each learner—whether reader, mover, or listener—is valued and important. This message, of course, is similar to the central message of the teaching-learning church: God loves all persons; each person is different and has unique gifts.

For many people learning connotes a formal setting such as a class or a study group, but we must not overlook the potential of informal settings. Learning can happen wherever there are persons receptive to the teaching-learning process. This is not a new idea, for in Deuteronomy 6:4-9 we read "Hear, O Israel: The LORD is our God, the LORD alone. You shall love the LORD your God with all your heart, and with all your soul, and with all your might. Keep these words that I am commanding you today in your heart. Recite them to your children and talk about them when you are at home and when you are away, when you lie down and when you rise. Bind them as a sign on your hand, fix them as an emblem on your forehead, and write them on the doorposts of your house and on your gates." What a wonderful reminder to take advantage of every opportunity for learning!

Many churches participate in camping programs for children and youth, but may overlook camping opportunities for senior adults, families, or adults of various ages. Many churches recognize the intergenerational nature of their congregation but may overlook the possibilities for intergenerational learning situations, such as a church retreat, an advent workshop, or a work-mission trip. Many churches enjoy music and drama in worship or special programs, but may not recognize the preparation and presentation as learning opportunities. Individuals and families may welcome audio and video cassettes with selections of Bible stories, movies, and presentations that stimulate thinking about Christian faith. Potential learning situations are all around us. The informality of a situation may be just what some learners need.

What Hinders Learning? What Encourages It?

Learning is hindered by fear of being wrong or not knowing enough, fear of change or not belonging, fear of dealing with difficult questions or being "put on the spot." There may even be the belief that one is "too old" or "too limited" to learn. To be in a learning situation is to acknowledge that one does not know everything. This may be one reason why it is often easier for children and youth to participate in learning situations.

Learning is also hindered by poor planning and the neglect of learners' needs and interests. Some persons carry memories of unpleasant learning situations and are reluctant to repeat the experience. These persons may learn best through touch or movement and have not been given that opportunity. These persons may have felt shut out when they raised questions or they may believe that the biblical message does not relate to what they are experiencing in life. The things that hinder learning are not insurmountable, but they do require attention when plans for learning are made.

The ways in which learning situations are planned and arranged can do much to encourage learning. When there is a climate of mutual trust and respect, when learners have freedom to express their ideas and questions, learning is encouraged. When persons are seen as more important than the information being taught and teachers are comfortable as learners, learning is encouraged. When there is provision for the physical comfort of learners (proper light, space, seating), learning is encouraged. When teachers are knowledgeable and supportive, when learners find enjoyment and value in the learning process, learning is encouraged.

Jesus said, "Go therefore and make [learners] . . . teaching them. . . . And remember, I am with you always, . . ." (Matthew 28:19-20). This the task of the teaching-learning church and the source of our power and encouragement.

Chapter 5

Functions of the Board

We can assume that the board of Christian education has responsibility for the total teaching ministry of the church, but this assumption creates some practical problems. The teaching ministry is only one of several ministries in the church. The others are proclamation, worship, fellowship, witness, and service. In fact, the teaching ministry undergirds all of the other ministries.

Sometimes determining the boundary line between the function of the board of Christian education and the work of other boards and committees is difficult. The following distinctions may be helpful:

1. There are some functions or programs that clearly belong to the teaching ministry, such as the work of the church school, the youth fellowship, vacation Bible/church school, through-the-week education, and so forth.

2. There are functions or programs in which teaching plays a subordinate role to the work of other boards and committees. For example, the worship life of the church and the conduct of service ministries in the community belong to this category. Such functions have educational components but the functions will be the responsibility of other boards or groups. In such cases, the board of Christian education may be called upon to provide assistance in relationship to the teaching dimensions of these programs.

3. All boards and committees—indeed, all persons within the congregation—have some responsibility for the unplanned, informal, and spontaneous teaching that takes place within the congregation. That responsibility includes both an awareness of the many informal ways in which a congregation teaches and individual efforts of persons to enhance the effectiveness of such teaching and learning.

This chapter will deal only with the first category—tasks that are clearly within the scope of the board of Christian education and for which it has the major responsibility.

In general, the board of Christian education formulates the policies of the church's teaching ministry and plans for the implementation of these policies. This function may be delineated more specifically in terms of the following responsibilities:

Understand the Task

Basic to understanding the task is an understanding of the concept of a teaching church. The board will find it helpful to use a part of its regular meetings to consider the implications of the material on a teaching church (chapter 1) and its learning stance (chapter 4). Reviewing the goal of the church's teaching ministry (chapter 2) and determining the purpose for that ministry (chapter 3) are essential elements in helping the board to understand its task. Models of organization are described in chapter 6.

Determine the Educational Program

A primary responsibility of the board of Christian education is to plan, implement, and evaluate the church's program of Christian education. Chapter 12 of this manual provides guidance for the board in relation to this process. Although the board may wish to include other boards, committees, and officers in the data gathering or other aspects of planning, the church will expect the board of Christian education to take the lead in planning and implementing the total education program.

Select Curriculum Resources

The board of Christian education acts for, and is responsible to, the church in determining the curriculum materials for its teaching program. The choice of a curriculum design and supporting curriculum materials is one of the chief functions of the board.

Choosing curriculum resources is a very important decision. It should not be left to a single individual, not even the pastor or the superintendent. The selection should not be made independently by each teacher. Such selection may result in a hodgepodge of resources. Rather, students, teachers, superintendents, and the professional staff of the church all need to be involved with the board of Christian education in the curriculum-selection process.

The significant factors to be considered in choosing curriculum resources include the goals that have been determined for the church school, the preferences of students and teachers, and elements of the teaching situation (such as the amount of time for class sessions and how children, youth, and adults are grouped in classes).

When a board is about to evaluate its present or a proposed curriculum series, it should first determine the appropriate questions that will serve as helpful guides in evaluating curriculum. Such questions will relate to the objectives, content, role of the teacher, teaching methods, artwork, and format of the materials. A "Selecting Curriculum" workshop, Self-Evaluating Questionnaire, and Selection Guides are available from Educational Ministries, American Baptist Churches-USA, P.O. Box 851, Valley Forge, PA 19482-0851, 1-800-4-JUDSON (1-800-458-3766). Most denominations have such helps available.

Enlist and Support Educational Leaders

A significant key to the effectiveness of the educational program is its leadership. It has been estimated that in the average church there is an annual turnover of from one-fourth to one-third of the leaders of the educational programs. The enlistment and support of leaders is a continual need.

The board of Christian education, through the person responsible for leader development, will want to develop a systematic plan for discovering, selecting, recruiting, training, and supporting leaders. Integral to such a plan is the concern for building a climate of motivation for leaders. What are the factors that motivate leaders? How can we recruit, train, and provide other support for leaders so as to contribute to their motivation? There are a number of helpful resources available to the coordinator of leader development and other persons responsible for the enlistment and support of leaders. See Appendix B at the end of this manual for a list of books that will be helpful to the person responsible for leader development.

Determine Job Descriptions with Leaders

Any leader is more likely to do a job well when the leader has had the opportunity to be involved in writing the job description for the position. A job description enables a leader to see what his or her job is. The descriptions are helpful tools for persons recruiting leaders. Job descriptions should be specific enough to be helpful to recruiters and open-ended enough to be revised by the leader and the person on the board of Christian education that he or she relates to as part of the orientation to the new position. Chapter 7 of this manual provides specific suggestions for developing job descriptions for educational workers in a church.

Prepare and Administer the Education Budget

Because teaching is a major ministry of the church, the expenses of the entire educational program of the church should be financed by the church budget. The board of Christian education should prepare an annual "asking budget," which will include all the projects and programs that the board plans for the year. (See sample, p. 24.) In developing the budget, the board should indicate two sets of figures, one showing the minimum requirements for the program and the other showing desirable additional funds. The budget committee can then prepare a total church budget, taking all interests into account. When the budget is later adjusted in light of church pledging, a realistic budget will be adopted by the church.

The board should administer the educational budget according to the policies of the church. It may be appropriate to appoint someone on the board with specific responsibility for budget administration. It may be helpful to the board to know at any time how much of the budget has been expended and how much is still available for use during the remainder of the year.

Allocate Space and Provide Equipment and Supplies

Students and their teachers or leaders are greatly influenced by the physical environment in which they meet. They respond to space, light, color, physical comfort, and freedom for creative activity. The board of Christian education is responsible for providing the best possible rooms and equipment as a setting for effective teaching and learning experiences.

The board should proceed on the assumption that a church building belongs to the whole church and that the church should decide how its building is to be used. If the

Sample Asking Budget

	Minimum	Desirable
The Sunday Church School (Curriculum resources and administrative expenses)	$_____	$_____
Vacation Bible/Church School	_____	_____
Mission Education (School of Missions, mission study tours or work projects)	_____	_____
Family Life Education (Itemize projects)	_____	_____
Intergenerational Education (Itemize projects)	_____	_____
Outdoor Education (Itemize projects)	_____	_____
Ministry with Children (Weekday nursery, after-school programs, etc.)	_____	_____
Ministry with Youth (Youth fellowship groups, retreats, conferences)	_____	_____
Ministry with Adults (Special study groups, retreats)	_____	_____
New Equipment	_____	_____
Multimedia Resources	_____	_____
Library	_____	_____
Leader Development (Scholarships for training events, cost of leadership classes, camperships)	_____	_____
Special Programs (Recognition dinner for the teaching staff, Loyalty Sunday, Rally Day)	_____	_____
Board Expenses (Administrative)	_____	_____
Miscellaneous	_____	_____
Totals	$_____	$_____

building is to be used in ways that best further its ministry, flexibility is needed so that the space can be redistributed from time to time to meet changing conditions, such as growth or decline in attendance.

Periodically, the board should conduct a survey of all equipment (including room decorations and furnishings), discard items that are obsolete or unneeded, replace or repair articles that are broken or out-of-date, and see that the educational rooms are attractive and clean. Major alterations or redecoration should be planned for the period of the year when classes or groups may have the lowest attendance.

It is essential that adequate supplies be provided for teachers and other educational leaders. These persons should not be expected to purchase necessary supplies themselves. Someone should be designated to be in touch with leaders regarding supply needs so that adequate materials can be on hand.

Interpret the Educational Program to the Congregation

The board of Christian education will interpret to the entire congregation the significance, objectives, and plans of the educational program. The purpose of such interpretation is to help persons recognize the importance of teaching in the ministry of the church and the responsibility of everyone within the congregation to be a growing person. The board will want to be alert to the varied ways in which they may develop an educational consciousness on the part of the congregation. Chapter 13 of this manual gives some specific suggestions related to developing congregational support, including possible methods for providing information about its educational ministry and programs.

Chapter 6

Models of Organization

Five models for structuring the administration of Christian education in a local church are outlined in this chapter. The first four models are related specifically to a board or committee of Christian education. The fifth model refers to a single-church-board structure. If your congregation administers Christian education more informally, pick and choose ideas from this chapter that will be helpful to your situation.

General Concerns

There are some general concerns that are common to any model for structuring the administration of Christian education.

A board of Christian education should include from three to twelve elected members, depending upon the size of the church. The following is suggested:

Under 100 members — 3 members
100 to 500 members — 6 members
500 to 1,000 members — 9 members
Over 1,000 members — 12 members

Members should be elected for a three-year term, with the terms of one-third of the board members ending each year. Board members will not succeed themselves in office after serving one or possibly two terms, without one year intervening. In addition to the elected members, there are persons who should serve by virtue of their office as ex-officio members with voting privileges. These members are the general superintendent of the Sunday church school, the pastor, and/or the minister of Christian education (or associate pastor with a Christian education portfolio) if there is one. The board should choose a chairperson and a secretary from among the elected members.

The suggested duties or responsibilities of the chairperson, secretary, Sunday church-school superintendent, pastor, and minister of Christian education in relationship to the board are considered in chapter 7.

If a church has a minister of Christian education (or associate pastor with a Christian education portfolio), there are special concerns that need to be considered. Such a person should be seen as staff to the board and its committees and task groups. This person should also be able to provide special support for teachers and other educational leaders. In addition, the church will need to look in detail at the roles of the minister of Christian education in relationship to the total educational needs of the church and to the roles of other paid professionals on the staff, including the pastor. It is important that both the pastor and the minister of Christian education be involved in planning and promoting the educational program of the congregation. The specific roles of each will need to be determined within a given congregation.

Selecting a Model

Each congregation will need to select the model for structuring the administration of Christian education that potentially will be most effective in its situation. A study of the possible strengths and weaknesses of the following models will enable a congregation to select the model that it prefers or to develop another model.

Model A: Board with Assigned Responsibilities

In this model every elected member is assigned a specific responsibility for some area within the church's ministry of Christian education. The possible areas of responsibility include:
General chairperson,
Coordinator of ministry with children,
Coordinator of ministry with youth,
Coordinator of ministry with adults,
Coordinator of leader development,
Coordinator of mission education,
Coordinator of family-life education,
Coordinator of camps and conferences,
Superintendent or coordinator of the Sunday church school.
There are a number of ways to make assignments to members. The importance of the different responsibilities will vary, depending on the makeup of the congregation and the priority given to each area of responsibility by the board. Furthermore, two or more lesser responsibilities can be combined and be considered the equivalent of one greater responsibility. Some possible patterns of assignment are described here.

If there are three members on the board of Christian education, each member should carry responsibility for one of the age-group functions (ministry with children, youth, or adults) and for one other area. Although several combinations are possible, one way of assigning responsibilities for the three members is:
General chairperson and coordinator of ministry with adults,
Coordinator of ministry with children and leader development,
Coordinator of ministry with youth and mission education.
If there are six members on the board, the board will need to make assignments of selected areas of responsibility, again on the basis of their priority for the congregation. One possible way of assigning these areas is:

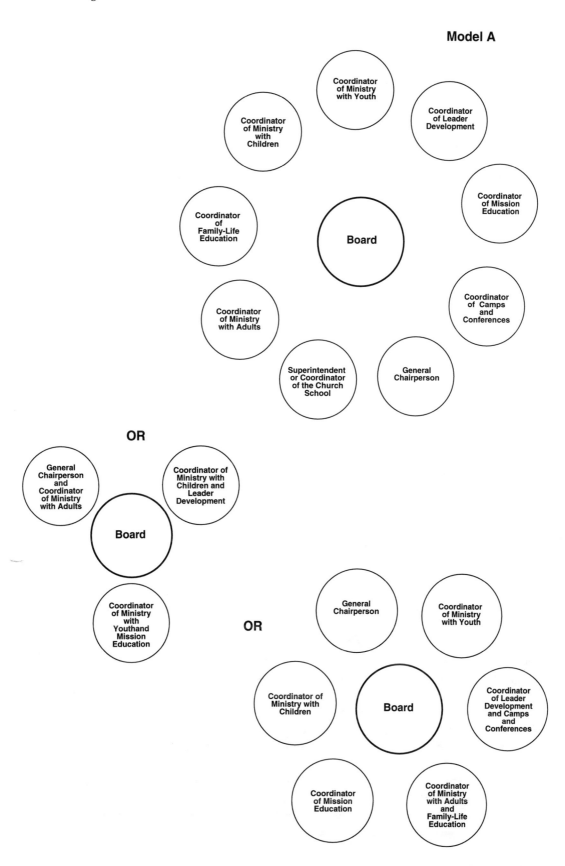

Model A

General chairperson,
Coordinator of ministry with children,
Coordinator of ministry with youth,
Coordinator of ministry with adults and family-life education,
Coordinator of leader development and camps and conferences,
Coordinator of mission education.

If there are nine members on the board, one member may be assigned to each of the nine areas of responsibility, or to some adaptation of the above listing. If there are twelve members on the board, other areas of responsibility may be assigned to some members. Regardless of the size of the board, assignments of responsibilities should be made on the basis of the priority of the areas of need within the church.

Specific duties and responsibilities for the general chairperson and coordinators on the board are suggested in chapter 7.

There are several values or strengths to this model. Each member on the board can work to become a specialist in the assigned area of responsibility. The model attempts to bring a balance to the board, with all important phases of the work of Christian education represented. Through the coordinators of ministry with children, youth, and adults there is a possibility of two-way communication between the board and age-group workers and leaders. Questions of a specific nature can be referred to the coordinators and consequently take less time on the agenda of the full board. It is possible that a member will serve more effectively and faithfully if a particular area of responsibility is assigned. The talents and "gifts" of persons can be matched to specific jobs as persons are elected to the board for specific areas of responsibility. The model can lead to clearer expectations on the part of the board and its members as to the roles and responsibilities of each person.

There are some cautions. It is possible that a concentration on a number of areas of responsibility can cause the board to lose sight of the "whole" or the total picture of Christian education. Furthermore, when a person is elected to an area of responsibility and fails to fulfill it, the board may not be able to pick up the slack for that area because of the responsibilities to which each member of the board is already committed.

Model B: Board with Assigned Responsibilities and Subcommittees

This model is like model A. What makes it different is that the coordinators function with or through subcommittees. In other words, the coordinator of ministry with children will work with and through a committee on ministry with children, which is appointed by the board. The subcommittee may be small (possibly three people) or large, depending on the size of the church and the assigned responsibility.

There are values or strengths in this model. More people can be involved in the work of the board as they are made members of subcommittees. The agenda of the board can be facilitated if committees meet separately and report their work to the board in the form of specific recommendations. The model is of particular value in larger congregations.

A caution should be noted. There is a danger that the board of Christian education in this structure could be just a rubber-stamping body, meeting simply to hear reports from subcommittees and to approve recommendations. It may be difficult for people to see value in attending such meetings.

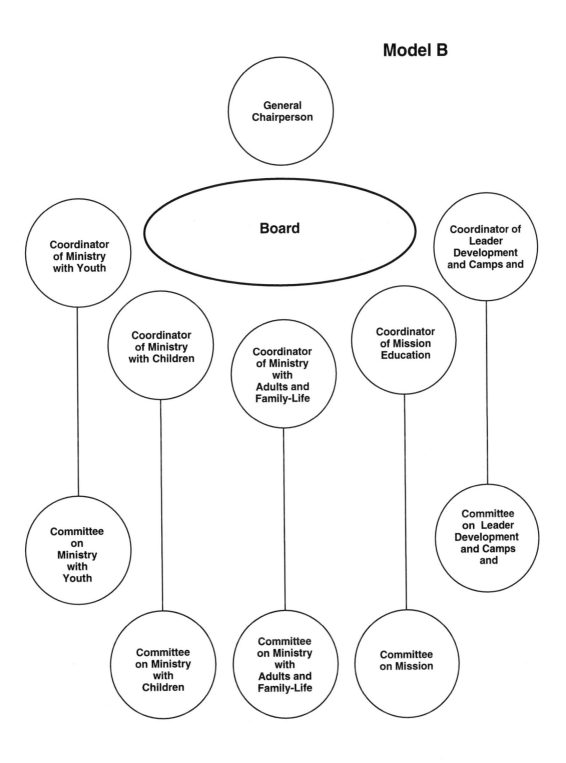

Model B

Model C: Board Operating with Task Groups

In this model the board of Christian education determines the programs and projects for the year. As a program or project is defined, a task group is appointed with responsibility for planning and implementing it. Members of the task group may be board members or persons outside of the board.

The task group is appointed to do a specific job within a given period of time. When the work is finished, the task group is dissolved.

The board may carry on its program entirely through task groups or with a combination of permanent committees and task groups. For example, there may be a permanent Sunday church school coordinating committee and a task group for rally day, a task group for the Christmas workshop, and so forth.

When a task group is appointed, the task should be important, meaningfully related to the objectives of the board, and relevant to current needs and priorities. The task should be clearly described and understood by members of the group. The time in which the task is to be accomplished should be specified and adequate. The number of persons in the group should be commensurate with the demands of the task—too few may not get the job done, and too many may be a waste of time and energy of members. The group should be composed of persons who have the necessary abilities and skills that the task requires. If not finished at its completion date, the task can be continued for an extended period, assigned to another group for completion, or discontinued. When a task is completed, the group should be disbanded.

There are several values or strengths in this model. It is particularly helpful in small churches with a limited number of leaders. In this model it is possible to utilize the resources of persons who are not willing to serve on a long-range basis in given tasks or regularly as a member of the board. The use of task groups provides a great deal of flexibility, because groups can be created as needed and go out of business when assigned tasks are completed. The use of task groups makes it possible to assign persons to responsibilities they are best fitted to perform.

There are cautions that should be made related to the model. It is possible that the use of task groups may require a great deal of time and effort in coordination. Detailed planning prior to the assignment of a task group and careful orientation of its members are essential. The board will need to look carefully at the total picture of the needs and possibilities of Christian education so as not to overlook or slight any given area, such as ministry with adults, mission education, and so forth.

Model D: Board with a Flexible Structure

In this model the structure may vary from year to year. In other words, the church may find it profitable to use model A for a period of time; circumstances may then change so that it is more profitable to use model B or model C for another period of time. Model D is particularly suitable for the board that uses a systematic planning process, that is, a board that carefully determines its overall goal for Christian education and its objectives and plans for the year and then asks what structure is needed in order to accomplish best these objectives and plans. At the heart of this model is the determination of the specific responsibilities of board members and others and the specific structure that will best help to achieve the objectives and plans.

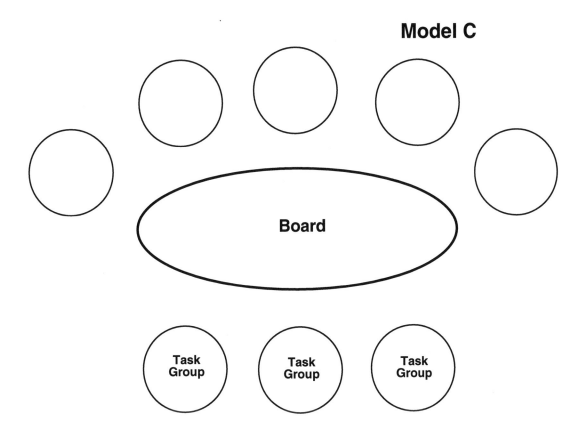

One of the strengths of this model is that the form of the structure is determined after the board has decided what it wishes to accomplish. This model allows more easily for changing roles and functions to be developed. The board is not locked into a given structure at a given time. Leaders can be reassigned as needed more easily within this model. The model allows for the possibility of careful deployment of the resources of leaders (skills, abilities, and knowledge) in relation to the teaching ministry.

Some cautions are in order regarding the model also. If careful systematic planning is not thoroughly done and implemented, the model will be ineffective. Careful evaluation is essential. There is the danger that too frequent a change in structure may make it difficult for leaders to feel secure in performing assigned tasks.

Model E: Church with a Single Board

Traditional structures of the free churches include several boards (for example, deacons, trustees, and Christian education), which meet monthly and whose programs are correlated through a church council. However, some churches prefer to function through a single church board that represents within itself all phases of the church's ministry. In this case there will be subcommittees of the board with designated, ongoing responsibilities. One of the subcommittees will be responsible for Christian education. In this case the subcommittee functions with much the same responsibility as a board of Christian education in a multiple-board structure.

Such a plan has some special values. It can insure correlation of all programs and make it possible to plan in terms of the total ministry of the church. Such a plan may have particular merit for use in the small church that has limited leadership resources.

One caution is important. The ministry of Christian education usually encompasses the largest number of program areas within a church. In other words, the group responsible for Christian education may be responsible for more programs than any other group within the congregation. If adequate time and personnel are not devoted to Christian education program planning, the educational ministry of the church may be shortchanged by the single-board structure. It is essential that persons who are appointed to the committee on Christian education of the single board have the knowledge, interest, time, and skills that will enable them to program for the ministry of Christian education.

Chapter 7

Job Description for Workers

Administrators of Christian education in a church know that the greatest asset of the program is the staff. Facilities, equipment, curriculum, and other factors can help or hinder the growth and ministry of Christian education, but none of these has nearly the potential, both positive and negative, that can be found in the leaders. The contributions that leaders can make depend on the leaders themselves as well as on their fitness for their particular jobs and their understanding of their duties. Job descriptions are helpful if leaders are to make their fullest contribution, but it must be understood that they are only tools.

A job description is a statement about (1) tasks to be done, (2) abilities and skills needed by the leader, (3) involvement of the leader in initial preparation time and additional meetings, (4) length of service in months or years, (5) working relationships with other persons, and (6) training required. Job descriptions should provide enough information for a person to function successfully and creatively in the position. It is helpful to connect job descriptions to the church's mission as well as to prospective leaders' skills and gifts. Job descriptions should encourage innovation. They should set the stage for success by the leader.

Reasons for Developing Job Descriptions

Job descriptions are valuable because they:
- help persons make a decision to accept a task;
- serve as a guide for the leader in fulfilling the position;
- are tools that help leaders to deal openly with expectations about assigned roles;
- are a helpful starting point for changing functions in order to meet changing individual or group needs, capacities, or goals; and
- offer a basis for evaluation.

Job descriptions are also related to the following factors:

The structure of Christian education. Several factors will determine how jobs are described, such as the size of the committee or group on which the leader will serve, whether the position is a coordinating one, and so forth.

Recruitment of leaders. The job description may be used by the recruiter to describe the job. It should be specific enough to be helpful but general and open-ended enough to be developed further as it is fulfilled. Such a description is essential when the recruiter and person being recruited are not familiar with the position.

Program priorities. As program priorities are determined for a given year, one or more job descriptions may need to be rewritten accordingly.

Personal goals of the leaders. What a leader really does may vary from what is expected by others merely because the personal goals of the leader vary from the expected goals of the board of Christian education. When persons are involved in the development of job descriptions, personal and job goals may be considered openly in an effort to eliminate such conflict.

Evaluation by leaders. A job description may be used by a leader in evaluating how well the task is being done. Periodic self-evaluation with each leader may result in improved effectiveness in reaching objectives.

Job Descriptions for All Leaders

The board of Christian education should first develop job descriptions for its own members. Each member of the board ought to be involved in describing his or her job in light of the needs of the church and the community and in light of personal skills and resources. When a person becomes a member of the board, he or she should have the opportunity to live with the written job description for a period of time and to suggest revisions to the board in light of personal skills, the needs to be met, and the priorities of the board. It is important for the board to experience the values of job descriptions for their own positions before such descriptions are prepared for other Christian education workers.

There should be a written job description for every leader appointed by the board of Christian education with responsibility for some phase of the church's teaching ministry. Some descriptions will be briefer than others because of the nature of the position. When the position descriptions are duplicated and shared with all the leaders, each one may benefit from the opportunity to see his or her position in relationship to the total leadership picture.

A Plan for Developing Job Descriptions

The plan for developing job descriptions, which will be suggested here, has several benefits, primarily because of the involvement of the leaders in the process of developing the job descriptions. This plan calls for a two-hour meeting in which all persons for whom job descriptions are being developed are included. Such a session may be held for writing job descriptions for members of the board of Christian education; for workers with children, youth, and adults; or any other group of educational leaders. Modify the plan as needed.

Prior to the two-hour session it is important for participants to be committed to the task of developing job descriptions. Although the session is certainly motivational in terms of fulfilling the job descriptions developed, there is need for some commitment to the process of writing job descriptions as the session begins. Furthermore, it is helpful for participants to review some written material related to their task prior to the session. For example, prior to a session in which members of the board of Christian education will be writing job descriptions for themselves, they may be asked to read portions of this manual.

Four steps are suggested for this session to write job descriptions.[1]

1. *Introducing the session.* The purpose and steps of the session should be explained.

2. *Writing job descriptions.* A sheet of large newsprint should be placed on the wall for each job description to be developed. Each sheet should be given a heading for the particular description to be written, such as: "Chairperson of the Board," "Sunday Church School Superintendent," "Primary Teacher," "Advisor of Junior High Youth Fellowship." The participants in a session will work in teams of two or three persons each. Each team will begin its work at one of the sheets of newsprint. They will be given three minutes to describe the tasks of the position. After three minutes, each team rotates to a second sheet. When a team rotates to the next sheet, it can add to the description already there, revise it, or delete portions of it.

It is important to remember that a job description will set forth the objectives, duties, relationships, length of service, and results expected of the person in the job. The team should be told to describe the job to be done, not the qualifications of the person for the job, for example, "Guide students in stimulating learning experiences," not "dedicated leader."

Three minutes should be allowed for each team to work at each of the sheets of newsprint. At the end of this task there will be a rough draft of a job description on each sheet of newsprint. The special importance of this step lies in the involvement of each leader in describing each position.

3. *Revising job descriptions.* During this step each leader will go to the sheet of newsprint that describes his or her job. There may be two or more persons at one sheet of newsprint, while there may be only one person at other sheets. Each individual or group will revise the newsprint description so they will feel comfortable in accepting and fulfilling the position. The importance of this step lies in providing the opportunity for leaders to indicate what they are willing to do in their assigned jobs. No leader does more than he or she is willing, no matter what a written job description may say about the position.

4. *Accepting job descriptions.* In this step the board of Christian education should discuss with each leader or group of leaders its job description as written on the newsprint. The descriptions may be revised further as this is done. Each description may be officially accepted by the board and the individual or group whose position is described. The importance of this step lies in the "contract" or agreement entered into by the leader or leaders and the board when each job description is accepted.

---

[1] This session is adapted from pages 30–31 of *Building an Effective Church School* by Kenneth D. Blazier (Valley Forge: Judson Press, 1976).

Sample Job Descriptions for the Board

Although each church is encouraged to develop its own job descriptions for all the leaders in the church's educational program in consultation with those leaders, members of boards of Christian education may be looking for suggestions related to the descriptions of their positions. The following descriptions of responsibilities for members of the board may be helpful. These descriptions are offered as examples. Tailor them to fit your situation.

Chairperson of the Board
- helps the board to develop an overall goal and specific objectives for Christian education and to work to achieve them;
- prepares an agenda for board meetings;
- presides as chairperson at board meetings;
- provides leadership in organizing the board and making assignments essential for implementation of objectives and plans;
- may serve as ex-officio member of all subcommittees and task groups of the board;
- represents the board on the church council or other official group(s);
- makes reports for the board to the church or church groups as necessary;
- guides in the preparation and supervision of the educational budget of the church.

Secretary
- keeps accurate minutes of board meetings;
- cares for correspondence for the board;
- keeps a system of records for the educational program.

Coordinator of Ministry with Children, Youth, and Adults
- recommends to and plans with the board a program to meet the needs of children, youth, and adults;
- assists in recruiting and training leaders for ministry with children, youth, and adults;
- facilitates the use of curriculum resources with children, youth, and adults;
- plans for special days or events for children, youth, and adults;
- builds good relationships with other leaders;
- oversees the teaching program in children's, youth, and adult classes of the Sunday church school, in cooperation with the church school superintendent;
- oversees the use of facilities and equipment;
- provides for evaluation of the program of ministry with children, youth, and adults.

Coordinator of Leader Development
- plans for an ongoing program of training for all educational leaders;
- arranges for leadership classes or workshops within the congregation;
- publicizes and promotes attendance in training events (workshops, conferences) held within the community or by the denomination;
- assists age-group coordinators in recruiting and orienting qualified personnel as leaders of educational programs.

Coordinator of Mission Education
- develops a year-round program of mission education for persons of all ages;
- oversees the development of mission education events, such as a School of Missions, a Family Mission Night, a mission study tour, a mission work project;
- recommends, develops, and oversees service projects approved by the board;
- encourages persons to be involved in mission projects within the community as well as overseas and to understand mission as reciprocal;
- encourages teachers and other leaders to use material interpreting denominational missions and mission emphases;
- promotes use of materials for the annual mission offerings of the denomination.

Coordinator of Family-Life Education
- develops a year-round program of family-life education;
- assists in recruiting and training leaders for ministry with families;
- supervises the development of family-life education events, such as a study group for parents, a family night gathering;
- encourages and assists teachers and leaders in incorporating family life concerns into the content of classes and groups;
- develops programs and promotion for annual Christian Family Week observances.

Coordinator of Camp and Conference Ministries
- interprets the values of camp and conference ministries to the congregation;
- promotes attendance of individuals and families in denominational camps and conferences;
- oversees the church's program of scholarships or other financial help for attendees;
- may plan retreats, camping experiences, or conferences for the church family;
- secures volunteer leadership from the congregation for denominational camp and conference programs;
- plans for reporting camp and conference experiences to the congregation.

Sunday Church School Superintendent or Coordinator
- administers the Sunday church school according to the policy of the board;
- acts as liaison between the board and Sunday church school staff;
- oversees the work of the Sunday church school staff in planning, implementing, and evaluating;
- reports regularly to the board regarding concerns, needs, and accomplishments of the school;
- recruits teachers and other workers with the approval of the board;
- works with the coordinator of leader development to develop, implement, and promote a teacher-training program;
- interprets the Sunday church school to the congregation;
- establishes a program for enrollment;
- secures persons to care for equipment and audiovisual materials and to handle other administrative details;
- acts as liaison with other church officers, boards, and committees regarding Sunday church school concerns.

Pastor (single-staff church) or Minister or Director of Christian Education or Associate
Pastor (multiple-staff church)*

- helps to coordinate the educational program with activities of other planning
  groups in the church;
- interprets the educational program to the congregation;
- gives leadership to particular educational goals and projects, as appropriate;
- assists the board in finding and challenging potential leaders for educational programs;
- helps to provide meaningful fellowship and worship experiences for the educational workers;
- works on a team with the chairperson of the board and Sunday church school
  superintendent to administer the total educational program of the church according to the policies of the board;
- helps the board to study and evaluate the educational program of the church;
- serves as a resource person to subcommittees and task groups of the board, en-
  couraging them to carry out their objectives and assignments;
- studies current materials on Christian education so as to be informed about available resources and possible goals and programs for the educational program of the
  church;
- helps the board to plan a long-range program of Christian education on the basis of
  the church's needs and to set directions.

---

* In multiple-staff churches the pastor and other staff members may share these tasks.

Chapter 8

The Board as a Group

A board or committee of Christian education is a group and, more specifically, a small group. As a small group, it has some defined characteristics, such as common criteria for membership. Members have a sense of common identity through their membership in the group and in the church. There are some common objectives for the group.

It is a task-oriented group; that is, the group has a job to do: planning, organizing, evaluating, and so on. But it cannot accomplish its task effectively without paying attention to its group life.

Every small group develops a life and distinctive character all its own. A basic issue in a small group's effectiveness is the kind of "personality" it develops. An effective group has a warm, cooperative, open personality. It supports its members and facilitates their work on the group task. The group will be productive to the extent that each member contributes in a productive way.

Since so much of what gets accomplished in the church's teaching ministry depends on the board and its functioning, what can be done to help the board be an effective small group?

First, the board needs to understand that an effective small group has two main functions: (1) a task function and (2) a group-maintenance function. Balanced attention to both functions is essential.

The Task Function

The task of a board is described in chapter 5 of this manual. Every church has its own unique needs. Each board must tailor a task description to fit its situation.

A written description includes:
- the church's goal and objectives for its educational program,
- the responsibilities assigned to the board,

- a description of designated roles and responsibilities assigned to individual members.

If your church has no such statement, the board can develop one, using the suggestions in this manual. An annual updating will help both new and old members to understand the board's task.

Each member needs to have a common understanding of the board's purpose and responsibilities in order to work effectively. When a person knows *what* the task is, he or she can then focus on *how* to get the task done.

Working at the Task

Some of the work of the board will get done in its meetings. Although board members soon discover that *most* of the work is done between meetings, effective meetings are essential for an effective board. It is important to recognize the characteristics of a good board meeting.

An effective board meeting:

- *is planned.* The chairperson will prepare a list of items to be considered, getting suggestions from board members, will propose a time schedule, and will indicate priority items.
- *includes a time of worship and/or prayer.* Responsibility for this may be shared among members.
- *follows orderly procedures.* A systematic order for dealing with the board's work helps members to prepare and to participate effectively. Regular, brief reports on the various facets of the board's work can keep members aware of their overall administrative task and role. Items that require further work should be listed separately from the reports.

  There will be an orderly process for making decisions. This does not necessarily mean following *Robert's Rules of Order.* An informal process that allows open discussion and decisions by consensus is often better for a small group. It is important for members to learn how to ask clarifying questions, to listen with openness, to offer summaries of a discussion, and to make a recommendation (or a motion, if appropriate). It helps also to have a member (besides the chairperson) who is willing to keep a watchful eye on the clock and "call time" when the agreed time for discussing an issue has ended.
- *records its work.* There will be a regular plan for recording reports, recommendations, and concerns.
- *clarifies assignments.* The work to be done before the next meeting or for other stated deadlines must be clearly identified and responsibilities assigned.
- *evaluates the process.* A brief look at the group process at the end of each meeting will result in more effective meetings. A quick sharing of what helped and what hindered a meeting can provide helpful clues for members. ("It helped to have Dick's report on newsprint so we could compare the figures." "Getting the minutes from last meeting early reminded me of my assignment.") Remember that much of what gets accomplished in a church's educational program depends on how the board functions. Members who share in evaluating their group learn through that process how to take responsibility for what happens in the group. A

checklist or a continuum such as the following can be answered quickly and followed up with helpful comments.

In getting our job done, this meeting was

1	2	3	4	5	6	7	8	9	10

Ineffective   *So-so*   *Effective*

The Maintenance Function

Task-oriented groups tend to overlook the importance of group maintenance. The usual tendency is to assume something like this: "We have a job to do; our time is limited; let's get on with it." Effective task groups have learned that attention to the life of the group helps them work more efficiently.

The group life of a board of Christian education has a very direct relationship to its work. Christian community is the context for faith education. Board members who are growing in faith through their experience of a caring, supportive group are motivated to plan a teaching ministry that nurtures the faith of others and demonstrates a caring concern for them.

A board provides for maintenance concerns and individual needs by:

• *clarifying expectations.* Members must have a sense of belonging and ownership. They need to know that their participation makes a difference and that it matters when they are absent or fail to follow through on assignments. Apathy does not develop in a group whose members feel needed and who know that they are accountable to others.

• *providing information and training* in basic group skills (both task and maintenance), such as how to listen, ask questions, summarize, deal with differences of opinion, relieve tension, and in areas of responsibility of board members.

• *allowing time for some personal sharing.* Individual burdens and concerns are lightened by knowing that others care. The board will have a greater sense of unity when members show that they care about one another, not just about the assigned tasks.

• *affirming God's presence.* It is assumed that boards will begin a meeting with a prayer for God's guidance. Such a practice can become routine and lose its meaning, however. Why not share the responsibility for the opening reminder of God's presence? Each member then has a chance to bring to the group's attention a pertinent Bible passage, prayer, reading, personal testimony of faith, or a stated hope for the church's educational work. Without such "reminder experiences" it is easy for board members to forget that their overall purpose is to help persons to grow in Christian commitment. It is essential to recall together that the accomplishment of that purpose ultimately depends on the degree to which God's power and presence are reflected in the lives of its members.

Chapter 9

Age-Group Concerns

A critical foundation stone of a teaching ministry is an understanding of the characteristics and needs of persons at every point in their life cycle and of the different ways persons learn at different times. Armed with such an understanding, the planner is better able to measure the adequacy of a total Christian education program.

Having a sense of what the issues are at the different age levels makes it easier to determine (1) what programs are needed in a congregation, (2) the varieties of leaders that are needed, and (3) the times in the lives of individuals when nurturing experiences may best result in Christian growth. Understanding the typical concerns of different age groups helps the planners of a congregation's teaching ministry more effectively equip that body of believers for mission.

Consequently, the human life cycle and its meaning for Christian teaching must be understood by planners. The Life Cycle chart will help us to look at the total span of human life, the various needs persons have at different times, and the ways persons learn as they grow older. The chart simplifies, of course, what is a complex process. No two people move through life at the same rate or according to the same pattern. The chart is only a tool. Its purpose is not to give an exhaustive account of human development but to identify major issues, patterns, and milestones that the planners of Christian education will find helpful.

The chart is organized into three levels: the innermost circle names some basic issues persons must face and resolve in order to grow; the second ring describes the different ways persons learn at different age levels; the third identifies the major chronological events in persons' lives. Some of the events listed are inevitable steps in the life cycle, common to all persons; others are listed as possibilities that may or may not occur. It is important to remember that individuals, racial-ethnic groups, and cultures vary in experiences and ways of responding to experiences.

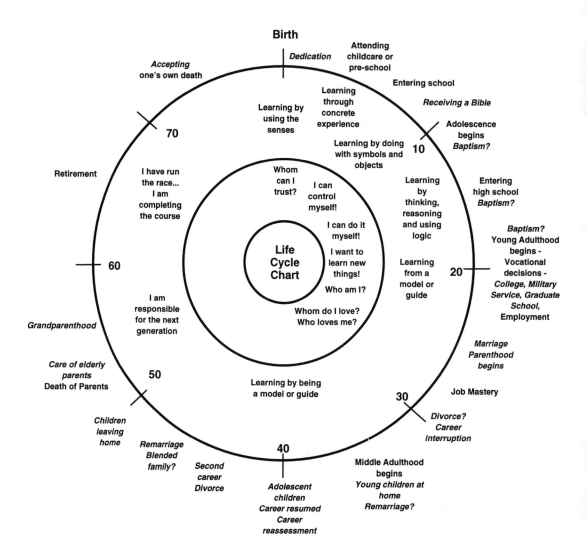

Italic type: possible experiences

Basic Life Issues

The young child (birth until about age five or six) must master three basic life issues, even while learning to crawl, talk, walk, use the toilet, and respond to parents, siblings, and others. "Whom can I trust?" points to the young child's radical dependence on others for survival and to what the child learns about being dependent. How trustworthy parents, church nursery caregivers, and other adults are will color a child's understanding of the trustworthiness of other people and of God. A basic attitude of trust or mistrust takes shape in this period.

The next hurdle for a young child is learning to be in control of oneself. Often this issue comes into focus around the experience of toilet training, but the issue is greater than that. The business of learning to walk and talk is part of this process. Learning to take turns and to help with simple tasks are among the ways a child learns to be self-controlled.

As the time for entering school nears, young children begin to want to tackle new experiences on their own. "I can do it myself" means taking initiative and testing limits. Children need a safe but challenging physical and social environment in which to try out their growing powers.

The school-age child is concerned with mastering new tasks and perfecting skills. Doing a thing well, matching a standard, and industriously doing "more than" are the ways school-age children grow in skill and self-confidence. Discovering that "I can contribute" is most important to the older child.

Adolescence is a time for defining and redefining who one is. The adolescent may "try on" different styles of personality in order to find a good fit. Many youth will be involved in "at risk" behaviors such as substance abuse, premarital sex, and so forth. The peer group grows in importance as the youth searches for a clue among peers to the question "Who am I?" Adolescence is "successful" when working answers to this question are found.

In *young adulthood* concern moves from "Who am I" to "Whom can I love and who loves me?" The basic issue is forming intimate relationships. Seeking and finding a life partner is often a major step in the process. A concern for mastery or achievement in the work world is often dominant in this period. "Who I am" is frequently translated "what I do." Struggling with the demands of job, on the one hand, and the need to invest in a significant relationship on the other is characteristic of young adults. Parenthood may begin in this period.

During *middle adulthood* the basic concern is to be a nurture giver, a provider, and a contributor to the welfare of the next generation. It is the time of job or career development and, typically, parenting. Whether the middle adult is single or married, a parent or a worker, it is a time of cultivating what one has created in physical and spiritual terms.

Later adulthood is characterized by a concern for comprehending and evaluating one's life. Employment is ending, and the last child has left the nest. Pulling together the strands of life into a whole and being able to affirm it is the goal of this period. It can be a time of satisfaction and contentment, especially if the tasks of the earlier years have been met with some degree of success.

Christian education across the life cycle needs to be planned with sensitivity to these basic life issues with which each one of us struggles as well as to societal issues and pressures such as the AIDS crisis. Transition times from one concern to another may well be times when persons are especially "teachable," open to the nurture of the faith community, and receptive to God's word for their lives.

Ways of Learning

Not only do the basic life issues that persons face change over a period of time, but also the ways in which persons learn can change. This is obvious with children. However, we are discovering that adults, too, learn in the context of different relationships at different times in their life journeys.

A Christian education program that seeks to match teaching-learning opportunities with intellectual, physical, social, and emotional development requires careful planning. Adult hopes to instill the Christian faith in children need to be matched with an appreciation for *what* can be learned at different age levels and *how* it can be learned. It is important to determine what an educated Christian should know about God, the Bible, and the heritage of our faith. It is equally important to identify when persons are ready for specific learnings. Good planning emphasizes both what ought to be taught and when it can best be learned.

But knowing God is more than having knowledge about God, the Bible, and the heritage of our faith, as helpful as that knowledge is. Knowing God is of the heart and soul as well as the mind. It comes from and grows stronger in and through personal experience.

In recent years we have also come to know that both individuals and cultures have differing learning styles. Some of us learn very well by seeing, others by hearing, others learn best via their sense of touch, and still others through any one of a mixture of ways of learning. Learning—how it happens—and learning in a teaching church are explored in more depth in chapter 4 of this manual.

Young children are action-oriented and sense-oriented. Abstract ideas do not move them. They can understand the birthday of the baby Jesus, his childhood, his kindness to others, and his trustworthiness. *Older children* can appreciate his role as a teacher and the wisdom of his sayings. They can conceive of God as a Creator. *Youth* can identify with Jesus Christ as a leader who sacrificed himself for his friends, and they can appreciate the concept of a God who has planned for the redemption of the world. While youth can often understand much of the complexity of theological concepts, it is usually true that the richness of theological symbols is most appreciated by *adults*, whose level of emotional maturity gives depth to their cognitive understandings. Younger adults, it is believed, are often in search of a model, a teacher, a guide, one who is able and willing to share the insights of experience. The most powerful learning takes place in this relationship. For the middle adult or older adult, learning comes through the experience of being the guide to someone younger. The potential of such relationships for Christian teaching and learning needs to be considered by planners.

Of course, *relationships* are at the heart of the Christian teaching-learning process at every stage and age. Younger children are not likely to remember the content of early Christian education experiences. They are likely to remember the context. The who of Christian teaching is often more important than the what. As persons mature and are able to grapple seriously with the content of faith, relationships remain the means by which content is communicated. The goal of Christian education is not only knowledge but a saving knowledge and a personal relationship to God in Christ. The quality of teacher-student or leader-participant relationships is crucial to reaching the goal.

Life Events

The outer ring of the chart identifies events in the life cycle. Many of these not only mark periods of growth in the development of persons and of crisis points along the way, but also indicate times when persons are especially teachable. For example:
- Parents may be especially receptive to training experiences when their children are born, enter school for the first time, or approach adolescence.
- Married couples are especially ready to learn communication skills six months or so after the wedding or when struggles occur.
- As children move from being able only to label things to being able to put them into novel combinations, they become ready to learn new concepts, such as the sequence of biblical events or the meaning of parables.
- Youth facing graduation from high school are more ready to achieve learning about vocation and the Christian's sense of "call."
- Single young adults may be ready for learning about the Christian meaning of love and friendship.
- Adults who are fifty-five years old may be more open to learning about retirement planning than adults of thirty-five.
- Times of crisis in a life, such as death of a loved one, divorce, serious illness, addictions, unemployment, are often times of readiness for change.

An Exercise

As members of a board of Christian education, take time to analyze the membership of your congregation and your program of Christian education in relation to the Life Cycle chart. Suggested steps:
1. Make copies of the Life Cycle chart for everyone on the board. (The chart may be duplicated in quantity for this purpose.) Feel free to add items to the chart that personalize it for your situation.
2. Write the following questions on newsprint or chalkboard:
   - Where are our members on the Life Cycle chart?
   - Do we find persons predominantly in one or two sectors or spread uniformly over the life cycle?
   - Are persons of the *same* age at *different* points in the life cycle?
   - Do we offer programs for persons in every phase of the life cycle?
   - Which of our programs focus or have focused on the turning points or crisis points in the life cycle or in individual's experiences?
   - Is there a part of the life cycle we are neglecting?
3. Allow ten minutes for individual work on the questions. You may find it helpful to provide copies of your church membership list. You might ask each one to draw a graph or a geometric shape that describes the distribution of your church membership across the life cycle.

4. Spend thirty minutes sharing observations. Try to reach a consensus about who the congregation is in terms of the life cycle and about where present programming is strong or weak.
5. Duplicate and share the Checklist of Needs and Gifts with the board. Permission to make copies of this chart has been granted to the users of this book. Discuss these questions:
    -   How many needs is your present program of Christian education meeting?
    -   Where in your program are you taking advantage of the gifts different generations have to contribute?
    -   How is the whole congregation being helped to understand and appreciate each generation?

Collate the responses to the checklist so they can be shared by the total group.

Checklist of Needs and Gifts

GENERATIONS	NEEDS AND CONCERNS	GIFTS
	(As you read these, what persons in your congregation come to mind?)	(What typical gifts would you add for each age level?)
Children Younger children (Birth to age 5 or 6)	☐ Food, sleep, protection, warmth, cleanliness ☐ Care, attention, response, holding, exercise ☐ Toilet training, acceptance of body ☐ Free exploration within limits ☐ Play with peers, expression of feeling ☐ Secure base of family support ☐ Variety of experiences	☐ Helplessness ☐ Charm ☐ Rapid growth ☐ Response to love ☐ Curiosity ☐ Openness in thoughts, feelings
Elementary children (Grades 1 to 5/6)	☐ Development of learning skills ☐ Exercise and coordination of large muscles ☐ Satisfying, self-directed work ☐ Dealing with success and failure ☐ Skill in peer group relations ☐ Experiences of care, service to others ☐ The challenge of ideas and self-investment	☐ Industry ☐ Rapid learning ☐ Vitality ☐ Imagination ☐ Expanding interests
Youth Early adolescents (Grades 6/7 to 8/9) Senior highs (Grades 9/10 to 12)	☐ Understanding and acceptance of pubescent changes ☐ Enriching peer relationships with both sexes ☐ Exposure to social issues ☐ Experiences of success ☐ Self-esteem, self-understanding ☐ Supportive adults, "adult guarantors" or mentors ☐ Increasing freedom and responsibility ☐ Opportunities to test roles, values, self-image ☐ Clarified values, sharper commitments	☐ Enthusiasm, passion ☐ Questioning attitude ☐ Loyalty to friends ☐ Idealism ☐ Physical strength, coordination ☐ Commitment to causes ☐ Growing competence
Young adults (After high school to 30 or 35)	☐ Responsibility for one's affairs ☐ Sense of vocational direction ☐ Close personal relationship with a few others ☐ Maturing relationship with one's parents ☐ Finding work, growing abilities in daily work; promotions ☐ Maturing sense of one's role in history/society ☐ Fidelity to loved ones ☐ Capacity to care for children	☐ Willingness to risk ☐ Expanding knowledge ☐ Creativity ☐ Intimacy
Middle adults (30/35 to 60/65)	☐ Financial security for one's family ☐ Marital adjustments ☐ Heavy demands of child rearing ☐ Creative, productive work in job and community ☐ Self-esteem in the face of disappointments, doubt ☐ Care and support for children in their new freedom ☐ Care of aged parents ☐ Exploration of new work and service options	☐ Dependability, steadiness ☐ Concern for the future ☐ Financial resources
Older adults (Over 60/65)	☐ Major adjustment to retirement ☐ Sufficient financial support ☐ Creative and useful investment of time ☐ Acceptance by persons and institutions ☐ Review and affirmation of one's life ☐ Human sharing in grief, joy, confusion ☐ Close relationships dwindling through death ☐ Increasing health care ☐ Limited mobility	☐ More time ☐ Wisdom, objectivity ☐ Person-centeredness ☐ Triumph over suffering ☐ Acceptance of death ☐ Hope

From *Learning Together: A Guide for Intergenerational Education in the Church* by George E. Koehler. Copyright 1977 by Discipleship Resources, P.O. Box 840, Nashville, TN 37202. Used by permission.

Chapter 10

Teaching-Learning Programs

Planners of Christian education need to focus on three types of programs:
* Ongoing programs that nurture all ages in Christian growth.
* Short-term programs that probe a particular experience or capitalize on a heightened readiness for learning in response to a life event. (See the Life Cycle chart in chapter 9.)
* Programs built around the church year.

Programs of Ongoing Nurture

Here are a number of program ideas, some familiar, some less so. Use this list to stimulate your own thinking.

1. The *"Sunday" church school* is probably the most familiar form of ongoing Christian education and nurture. The church school has many strengths, not the least of which is its long tradition. All ages potentially can be a part of the church school. It is frequently the point of entry into the church family and provides the structure for those small-group experiences that help people to feel they belong to the church. Usually the church school provides a graded experience so that the ways of learning and basic life issues of each age group can be fully respected and directly addressed.

2. A variation on the church school is an *after-school group.* Here the focus is often on Bible study, group activities, and recreation in a peer setting. A chance to reach out to the unchurched in the neighborhood is one attractive feature of an after-school group. Many churches provide study centers or tutoring in after-school groups or offer a latch-key program for children of working parents.

3. *Vacation Bible/church school* presents another time and place for Christian education. The greater informality of vacation time means an opportunity to enjoy games, "messy activities," and the outdoors. There is the potential for reaching unchurched neighborhood people. A great variety of vacation church school structures and times

have been introduced in recent years. One variation on vacation church school is an intergenerational model involving all ages and entire family units. Another summer option is day camping.

4. *Nursery school and day care* are two increasingly significant programs through which churches can provide nurture to children and their families. As the proportion of mothers who are employed outside the home has grown and as single-parent families have become more visible, the potential for ministry through nursery and day-care programs has become more clear. An important variation on this theme is special educational programs for children with disabilities. Early intervention in the lives of children with learning or physical disabilities is now understood to be a critical need. Churches are one obvious place to house such programs; often churches can and do take the initiative to create such vital ministries to the community.

5. Another familiar form of ongoing education and nurture is the *youth fellowship group*. Adolescents gravitate to peers because of their basic needs. The church has long responded to this need by creating youth groups, peer associations in a Christian framework. Variations on the traditional Sunday evening fellowship include small discussion or Bible study groups meeting weekly in homes, a plan of regular weekend retreats for a concentrated experience, recreational programs and teams, and special ministries with young men or young women.

6. *Camp and conference programs and retreats,* either under denominational sponsorship or under the direction of a local congregation, are another important style of ongoing nurture. The residential nature of camp, conference, or retreat provides an intense experience in Christian community unavailable in any other setting. Trail and trip camps can help persons discover new strengths and learn new skills. Camps and conferences can respond to all age groups, from infants brought by parents to family camp to senior citizens. Camps can be designed for persons with disabilities as well and offer an opportunity to discover new levels of personal resources, new depths of interpersonal relationships, and new visions of God's kingdom. Retreats can realize some of the same values in a shorter time period.

7. *Adult groups* of all kinds are another important program category. Ongoing adult fellowship groups, auxiliary groups, ushers, Bible study groups, couples' clubs, senior citizen fellowships, and separate groups for men and women deserve consideration as ways to do Christian education. Adults are both interested in and equipped to tackle serious theological questions, such as "What is the Christian meaning of suffering?" "What or who gives to my personal life a sense of perspective, value, and order?" Adult groups provide their members with ongoing support, a safety net in a crisis, and a fellowship of learning for personal growth.

8. *Family groups* are a way to minister to the whole life cycle. Families can learn from one another. Both parents and children are helped to understand each other better by seeing the various ways people relate in different families. Some churches have established family-life centers.

9. *Issue forums and mission study* are vital to a balanced educational ministry. Ongoing programs of mission education, forums for discussion and consciousness-raising about major issues confronting the community, and regular opportunities for youth and adults to engage in careful study of such serious problems as prejudice, justice, hunger, poverty, militarism, energy use, and human rights can be part of a relevant and life-changing program of Christian education.

Programs in Response to Teachable Moments

This list is certainly not complete. It is offered to stimulate a broader vision of the possibilities for educational programs.

1. *Marriage enrichment* is a periodic need recognized by an increasing number of couples. A marriage enrichment program is typically a weekend experience focused on helping couples to communicate better and appreciate each other more. There are many forms of marriage enrichment. Consultation with denominational family-life staff is recommended to determine the style most appropriate for your congregation.

2. *Sexuality education* for older children, youth, and adults is another need that can be met through periodic programs. Congregations that provide sexuality education experiences for adults have better participation and greater support for sexuality education programs aimed at older children and youth. One important aspect of adult sexuality education is preparing parents to be more effective sex educators.

3. *Parent education* is another major area for specific short-term training. Parents may be particularly open to educational experiences when their children are born, when their children first enter school, and when their children become adolescents. Major content and skill areas to focus upon include communication skills; understanding the physical, mental, emotional, and spiritual development of children and youth; problem solving; and conflict resolution.

4. *Intergenerational events* are another kind of periodic program that can make a large contribution to the vitality of a congregation. As the Life Cycle chart suggests, the generations have much to contribute to one another's growth and development. Intergenerational events can have a celebratory, nurturing focus as well as an educational focus. There are learnings that cannot be achieved in any other setting. The potential of intergenerational experiences for building the sense of "family" in the congregation makes this a most attractive kind of program. The increasing availability of resources for intergenerational education makes it easier to plan such events. Intergenerational education is an approach that can be used for programs of ongoing nurture as well. It is usually helpful to introduce intergenerational education in a short-term experience to lessen resistance to doing something new—for instance, trying an intergenerational summer church school, school of missions, vacation church school, or advent or lenten series.

5. Adult developmental crises provide occasions for *short-term, adult educational groups.* Topics such as the ever-changing male-female roles, aging, death and grief, divorce, unemployment, second careers, and retirement can be the focus for adult learning-nurturing groups.

6. *Issue education-action* groups are another kind of sharply focused, limited-term experience that has an important role to play in educational ministry. In response to a community concern or crisis, both youth and adults can learn about and contribute to the resolution of issues. Outreach ministries are often born of study groups focusing on a problem concerning the larger community beyond the church family.

7. *Groups for persons of special need* are another important way a church nurtures and educates. Groups for children in crisis, single parents, the recently divorced or widowed, parents of children or youth with developmental disabilities, recovering drug or alcohol abusers, and abusive parents or battered spouses can be a vitally important outreach ministry, Often a church will cooperate with other agencies in the development of

such programs. A church communicates the gospel in telling ways when its caring takes form in groups like these.

8. *Preparation for church membership* is a periodic, important, and joyful responsibility. Older children, youth, and adults, with their varying needs, understandings, and questions deserve careful attention as they prepare to make a public affirmation of faith or to join the congregation by letter.

9. *Learning to use the Bible* is especially important when third or fourth graders first receive Bibles from the church. This special occasion may well raise a youngster's motivation to explore and use the Christian community's special book.

10. *Using board and committee meetings* to build a working team, improve skills, and understand assigned ministry can help these groups become more effective.

11. *Intensive Bible study* is sought by many adults. Many churches offer Kerygma programs for these adults.

Programs in Response to the Church Year

One way to organize educational programs is around the church year. The basis for organizing the church year is the life of Christ but other events representing the church's history and current life can be added—such as special days honoring ushers, women, men, youth, graduates, etc. The following are all possibilities.
   1. Advent and Christmas
   2. Student Recognition Sunday
   3. New Year's Eve/Day
   4. Martin Luther King, Jr.'s Birthday (January)
   5. Lent
   6. World Day of Prayer (March)
   7. Palm Sunday
   8. Maundy Thursday
   9. Good Friday
   10. Easter
   11. Holocaust Day
   12. Peace Sunday
   13. Family Week (May)
   14. Pentecost
   15. Religious Liberty Sunday (June)
   16. Children's Day (June)
   17. Christian Education Sunday (September)
   18. World Communion Sunday (October)
   19. Reformation Sunday (October)
   20. Thanksgiving (November)

Chapter 11

Volunteer Leadership Plan—
A New Image

"Volunteer ministries are the heart of the church. It is through involvement and service that we discover and share the best we have to give. It's what brings our theology to life. It's how we recognize the Christ in others and ourselves."[1]

This statement offers an understanding that we can affirm without hesitation. Realistically, it may speak more of what we would like to see in volunteer leadership than what actually exists. A consideration of volunteer leadership in the church today would seem to indicate that we are face-to-face with a dilemma, if not a crisis. Some people say that our society has changed and that volunteers are no longer available. Other people suggest that the church has failed to keep up with the current theories and practice of volunteer involvement. The most pointed criticism says that the church is guilty of volunteer "abuse" through such practices as:

- poorly describing responsibilities,
- assuming service for "eternity,"
- providing little or no support,
- lacking purpose or accomplishment,
- offering little or no affirmation.

So whether the leadership dilemma is caused by poor practices in the church, changes in the culture at large, or both, what can we do to create an new image? In this chapter we will explore some issues of volunteer leadership and what we can do to create a contemporary understanding of volunteer roles and needs in the church today. It includes steps that can be taken to bring about a "new day" for the involvement of volunteers in the ministry of the church—a leader development plan.

---

[1] Margie Morris, *Volunteer Ministries—New Strategies for Today's Church* (Sherman, Texas: Newton-Cline Press, 1990), 14.

Who Are Leaders?

When we talk about leaders in this chapter we are not talking about a chosen few, just those persons defined as leaders by the church's constitution. We are talking about a much broader population. The following understanding of a leader suggests that everyone can be involved.

"A leader is a person who uses her or his gifts to enable [help] others in ministry."[2]

With this definition the following would be included as leaders:
- pianists and pastors,
- odd-job doers (such as the person who puts new attendance cards and pencils in the pew racks) and moderators,
- flower arrangers and committee members,
- teachers and those who prepare meals.

All of the above people are using their gifts to help others in ministry. So think of everyone as having either a leadership function or leadership potential. Leadership, in varieties of ways, is something all of us can be about.

Throughout this chapter you will find the terms *volunteers, leaders,* and *volunteer leaders* used interchangeably. Please remember each refers to the same people—volunteer leaders in the church. While the focus is on leadership within the church, we are aware that leaders are prepared in the church for leadership outside and most persons do both. The printed page limits the extent of our focus in ways that our imagination need not be limited.

We Need a Plan!

We need leadership development plans because having effective leadership is not an accident. It does not just happen in our congregations. While we need to be open to the Spirit of God at work in our midst there are some steps we can take to have more effective and vital leaders involved in the ministry of the church of Jesus Christ.

Leadership plans do not develop in a vacuum. Most churches have a way of doing leadership development that may have been in place for years and may not have been identified as such. It is just the way it is done. So if you are trying to institute a new way of doing leadership development remember that leadership life has gone on before and is going on now. Take that into account as you plan for changes.

Following are nine steps in a leadership plan. There is a brief discussion of what needs to happen in implementing each step. The development of each step of the plan is left up to the thinking and creativity of individuals and the appropriate board or committee in your church. Modify the plan to fit your situation.

The plan includes the following steps:
1. Explore Jesus' model of leadership.
2. Create a positive leadership atmosphere.
3. Build ownership.

---

[2] Jeffrey D. Jones, "The Meaning of Leadership" *Baptist Leader,* April 1981 (Valley Forge: Educational Ministries, ABC/USA), 36.

4. Deal with the issue of length of service.
5. Identify the leadership skills of all members.
6. Recruit persons.
7. Provide motivation and support for leaders.
8. Affirm leaders.
9. Involve leaders in evaluation.

Step 1: Explore Jesus' Model of Leadership

Volunteerism is implicit in the New Testament. Philippians 2:5-8 suggests that we be like Jesus who even "though he was in the form of God" did not seek equality with God. Rather he became a slave, a servant—"he humbled himself and became obedient."

A current resource on volunteerism suggests that "Jesus volunteered. He voluntarily became a servant to provide us with an example of what God expects." The model is established. The pattern is in place. The disciples were volunteers; the seventy were volunteers; the leaders of the early church were volunteers.[3]

Luke 4:18-19 offers the first job description for volunteers: preach the good news, proclaim release and recovery, set at liberty, proclaim the acceptable year of the Lord. The source quoted earlier elaborates on this passage. Most helpful are the comments on "the acceptable year of the Lord." "This refers to the year of Jubilee, a once in every fifty years celebration when all debts are canceled, a time of great rejoicing. Volunteerism may help people cancel their spiritual debts, their physical debts, and their emotional debts to others. Volunteers share in the jubilee by paying some of their indebtedness to society and perhaps even help compensate for wrongs they have committed by making restitution through their service. Those who give of their time often receive great joy from their efforts, constituting a celebration of jubilee among volunteers."[4]

Finally 1 Peter 2:9 describes all Christians as persons responsible for doing ministry—not just the pastor or the elected leaders, but all persons. Here we are all charged with ministry. Expressed in today's language, we are all volunteers involved in ministry.

Step 2: Create a Positive Leadership Atmosphere

Talk leadership whenever you get the chance! Talk about:
• the nature of leadership,
• leadership in relation to discipleship,
• the constantly changing leadership needs of the church,
• the need to support leadership.

Leadership—information about and an understanding of—should permeate every facet of church life. Understanding the ideas of leadership in general and one's personal relationship to leadership needs is the goal to be achieved in a pro-leadership atmosphere. Such an atmosphere, where leadership is understood, will be a place

---

[3] Donald Ratcliff and Blake J. Neff, *The Complete Guide to Religious Education Volunteers* (Birmingham: Religious Education Press, 1993), 15.
[4] *Ibid.*, 16.

where openness to the possibilities of giving leadership will be received in an increasingly positive way.

What a change that can be from a setting where the initiation of any leadership question provokes defensiveness, excuses, and the reduction of leadership needs and images to the lowest common denominator. This occurs when leadership is sought with such comments as:

"It won't take much time."

"You don't have to attend all the meetings."

"Your experience will make it easy."

"Just do it for this year."

Such statements often are made with the implication that "we've tried everyone else!"

So talk about the matter of leadership—through the preaching ministry, in church school classes, in board and committee meetings, with people who should consider their leadership gifts, with new member classes, and with special groups invited to consider the meaning of leadership. Be intentional and consistent in talking about leadership. Such conversation can change things.

Step 3: Build Ownership

Ownership is the term used when members of any group can say because of their involvement that this is **my** group, **my** church. "My" is a declaration of ownership.

Ownership is the foundation for the creation of a positive leadership atmosphere in a congregation. A sense of ownership helps members of a congregation realize that they can participate in setting direction for their church. Such an understanding will demonstrate for potential leaders the possibility of satisfying accomplishment as a leader. Ownership is not built overnight. It grows and builds over time.

Possible ways of achieving ownership:
- Have an all-church planning retreat that is "all church" and not just for officers.
- Ask the whole congregation for opinions about program activities.
- Demonstrate that congregational opinions are valued.
- Have a planning committee use subcommittees for greater participation in planning parts of a program.
- Have a member of a planning group call church members to seek their response to a program idea.
- Rotate planners in order to involve more people.

Ownership is enhanced when members of a congregation:
- join in identifying problems, concerns, and possibilities,
- participate in setting goals and objectives,
- plan ways to accomplish goals and objectives,
- are involved in implementation.

The results of ownership:
- More people are involved.
- More people are stating their ideas.
- The leadership atmosphere in the church is enhanced.

- Leaders have authority and accountability to make decisions about the work they are doing.

Building ownership is an ongoing process. What is developed in this step is just a beginning. The work and cultivation of ownership continues. Ownership, evidenced by an increasingly positive attitude about leadership and an accepting atmosphere, is a good starting point.

Step 4: Deal With the Issue of Length of Service

One of the major roadblocks to persons accepting invitations for leadership is the image they have of the requested role lasting "for eternity." This is particularly true of Christian education positions and other roles not controlled by a constitutionally mandated period of service and rotation policy. Even having constitutionally set lengths of service has not solved the problem. We need to think about "how long..." in new terms. Words and terms such as length of service, reassignment, sabbaticals, retirement, and even termination need to be part of our thinking.

Length of service is an important issue. When inviting a person to assume a volunteer leadership position it is appropriate to indicate when the responsibility will start and when it will end. It is crucial to maintain both of these times, particularly the ending date. Ignoring the date or even extending it gives credence to the opinions of many people that acceptance of a leadership role is an "eternal commitment."

In thinking about length of service we need to recognize that traditions of two- or three-year terms or a full year of service as a church school teacher may be deterrents to acceptance. People may be able to give short periods of time but are unable to make long-term commitments. We need to be flexible. Such flexibility will make for more effective utilization of the leadership resources that are available to a church.

Churches are occasionally faced with questions related to a leader or teacher who has served too long and lost his or her effectiveness. Often there is evidence that tasks are only partially completed or not done and the response to the leader is declining. When such a situation occurs there seem to be two possible options:

1. Confront the person, ask him or her to resign, and risk alienating others in the church who do not realize the problem being addressed.
2. Live with the situation and risk alienating those in the church who do realize the problem.

Whichever of these options is chosen, it should assure for the individual involved that spiritual growth, understanding of leadership, and development of leadership skills will continue.

This dilemma can be avoided by establishing a church-wide policy (a norm or standard) that all leadership roles in the church are for a specific time frame. Such an agreement implies that when a person completes an agreed upon period of service as a leader that he or she:

- will celebrate what has been done and acknowledge completion,
- move to another leadership responsibility in the church,
- go on "sabbatical" for personal renewal, being open to another responsibility at a later date,
- retire from leadership responsibility, or

- in exceptional cases continue for an additional period of service under a mutual agreement.

If a volunteer is failing to work toward the goals and objectives agreed upon, is negligent in performance and is not doing the job, we can terminate the volunteer. "It's just not done," you say. "After all, he or she is a volunteer—not a paid employee." Volunteers are not free to do just as they please. Such behavior is detrimental to volunteers, those with whom they are working, the program, and the ministry of the church. Volunteers can be held accountable.

"Obviously, prevention is the best solution. When our volunteer ministries are proficiently managed, careful placement is a top priority. If a problem does occur, thoughtful dialogue and a mutual plan to correct the situation are often all that is needed. When such steps fail, we have no recourse except to talk honestly with the volunteer and suggest other areas of service.

"There is always the danger that the person will take offense and leave the church. Nobody likes to see that happen. There is a place of service for everyone. But we can't control another's response."[5]

Establishing and maintaining set periods of service for leadership responsibility will provide greater assurance that the ministry of the congregation will increase in effectiveness and that the personal growth of the leader will be enhanced.

Step 5: Identify the Leadership Skills of All Members

Earlier in this chapter we made the bold assumption that everyone can lead. Everyone does not lead in the same way or give leadership to comparable activities. Some persons' gifts will equip them to serve as moderators or chairpersons. Others possess gifts that are best suited for behind-the-scenes activities that support other leaders. That, too, is leadership. This broad understanding of leadership is not present in all churches. If it is not present in your congregation, you will need to foster such a climate.

This step calls for the identification of the leadership gifts and skills of all members of the congregation. This task can be assigned to a leadership coordinator or to the chairperson or members of the leadership committee of the board of Christian education (or in some churches the nominating committee). The task of this person(s) would be to understand the leadership potential of every member of the congregation and to identify places or roles for which persons might be considered for leadership.

Rather than starting with a list of positions, start with people—their gifts and skills—and a desire to respond to their needs and interests. If the congregation has not been involved in a spiritual-gifts assessment or inventory,[6] it would be a good idea to do that

---

[5] Margie Morris, *Tools for Building Your Volunteer Ministry* (Sherman, Texas: Newton-Cline Press, 1992), 66.

[6] One spiritual gifts inventory available is *Discover Your Gifts* (Grand Rapids: Christian Reformed Home Missions, 1983). Leader's Notebook ($35.00), student workbook ($4.95) available from Christian Reformed Church in North America Home Missions, 2850 Kalamazoo S.E., Grand Rapids, MI 49560, (616) 246-0772.

before proceeding with this step. If members of the congregation have completed spiritual-gift inventories, use this information as the base for the following substeps:

1. Build a list of the members and friends of the congregation identifying the leadership gifts of each person.
2. Interview members of the congregation. Indicate that the church is seeking to discover the leadership resources available within the congregation. The following are examples of questions that might be asked in an interview.
   a. What would you like to do in a leadership role to help accomplish the mission of our church in the coming year?
   b. If you personally could design the leadership role you would be willing to assume, what would it look like?
   c. What would it take for giving leadership to the church to be important and fulfilling for you?
3. Write up a brief report of each interview.
4. Review the results of the interviews, connecting specific persons with possible responsibilities.

Finding and involving leaders for most churches often is a "seasonal" activity. In the spring or fall, depending on the church's fiscal or calendar year, the nominating committee takes on the task of filling in the constitutionally mandated slots. In the summer or early fall there is the "annual scramble" to recruit teachers and youth leaders. We need to move from a seasonal approach to an ongoing process, evident through the year, in which the identification and involvement of new leaders is a daily concern.

Step 6: Recruit Persons

"Your church wants you to be a satisfied and growing disciple of Jesus Christ." This is what the leadership coordinator, chairperson, or members of the leadership committee or nominating committee should communicate in the recruitment process.

Recruitment needs to be person-centered in contrast to program-centered. In this process we need to recognize that persons have specific reasons for volunteering and that our responses to these reasons will help them make a positive response to a leadership invitation. The reasons include:
- a need to participate,
- an opportunity to serve in the ministry of the church,
- the possibility of accomplishment,
- the desire to learn,
- an opportunity to be creative,
- a need to be heard,
- an opportunity to learn and grow.

When there is a leadership opening and a person has been matched to the responsibility, have a member of the leadership committee contact the person again, asking her or him to accept a responsibility. Indicate:
- why the person is being asked,
- what the responsibilities are,
- how much time it will take,
- when the responsibilities begin and end,

- what the leadership committee believes will be the personal satisfactions the individual will receive for doing the job.

Ask the individual if he or she can give a response to the request now, or if not now, by a time mutually agreed upon.[7]

It is important to recognize that volunteer leaders are not pawns in a game. They are people who, when respected, provide amazing service.

In the recruitment process the leadership committee should be prepared to offer a specific job description to each prospective volunteer. He or she deserves the right to clearly understand what will be expected prior to making a decision. Chapter 7, "Job Descriptions for Workers," offers guidance in developing job descriptions for positions of leadership in the church. You will also find sample job descriptions in a book listed in Appendix B, Resources: *How to Mobilize Church Volunteers*.

Step 7: Provide Motivation and Support for Leaders

Support is key in maintaining leader involvement. Factors that assure support include: a sense of accomplishment, personal growth, positive relationships, ability to influence, and being affirmed. These are among the behaviors that most contribute to a person's motivation to stay with a volunteer leadership responsibility.

Support begins with the manner in which a person is identified and invited for a volunteer leadership responsibility. If recruitment is done in a positive way, reflecting the degree to which the individual is valued as a person, support will have been initiated. Providing a job description is also a way to offer support. The description should indicate the nature of the support that will be given, when and how it will be offered, and who will provide it.

1. Support is offered by the very tone and behavior of a congregation that is leader sensitive.

2. Support is offered when leaders and their roles are regularly interpreted in the church newsletter, in other communications, and in worship or other activities.

3. Support is offered when pastors, other professional church leaders, the moderator, and church officers initiate conversations with leaders asking, "How's it going?"

4. Support is offered when growth opportunities are offered regularly and in a variety of ways. Growth opportunities are possible right in one's own congregation through:

- individual reading (see Appendix B, Resources for recommended reading);
- guided reading followed by conversation in a group;
- group meetings where such questions as, How are we doing in our leadership function; how can we adjust or correct our course; how can we be supportive of each other; and how can we grow together as a group while we fulfill our responsibilities? can be asked;
- selection of a specific time in the year for planned growth opportunities. It can be thought of as a "season for leader development." One time block in the church's

---

[7] Adapted from "Notes to Church Officers," John L. Carroll, *Baptist Leader*, Spring 1993 (Valley Forge: Educational Ministries, ABC/USA).

program year that is relatively open is January 1 to Ash Wednesday. In a "season for leader development" workshops might be offered on a specific evening or day for six weeks; concentrated in a one- or two-week period; offered through a weekend retreat followed by one or more weeknight sessions.

- Growth opportunities (conferences, seminars, workshops) offered by national and regional structures of denominations. Contact your denominational office for information.

5. Support is offered when growth opportunities are supported financially by the church. Volunteer leaders should not be expected to "pay their way." Financial support by the congregation is a statement of affirmation and support. Include a leader development item in the church budget.

6. Support, and therefore motivation, for current, ongoing, and future responsibility as a volunteer leader are extended when a volunteer leader is invited to offer constructive evaluation of the service rendered.

Support is not simply an occasional pat on the back, nor is it simply a word of thanks given at the end of an individual's service. Support must be continual and all-pervading. The tendency for frustration and resignation is reduced, if not eliminated, when a supportive climate is in place in the congregation.

Step 8: Affirm Leaders

Say thank-you in every way possible. Many thank-yous are implicit in what has been said so far in this chapter. Affirmation is twofold:

- First, affirm the person as one who is valued and of worth, for the gifts he or she possesses and offers to both the congregation and the larger community;
- Second, affirm the job being done.

Affirmation is not simply an end of the job activity. Don't save all your thank-yous for the moment of completion.

- Say thank-you and affirm the person in the process of recruitment.
- Say thank-you personally and individually throughout the period of service
- Say thank-you regularly and routinely in worship services, at other congregational events, and through the church newsletter by first introducing persons new to leadership assignments and then at a later date by reporting on the status of their work.
- Have a quarterly commissioning of persons new to leadership assignments as part of a worship service, just as we dedicate or baptize infants and welcome new members.
- Say thank-you by having a leadership roster in the church directory or on an attractive bulletin board in a high traffic area, perhaps even with pictures.
- Say thank-you by recognizing satisfactory completion of service.[8]

---

[8] Marlene Wilson in her book *How to Mobilize Church Volunteers*, (Minneapolis: Augsburg Press, 1983) suggests many more ways to recognize volunteers. You may want to refer to this book.

Step 9: Involve Leaders in Evaluation

"Did I do what was expected of me? Was my work perceived as satisfactory—even exceptional? Or, did I miss the mark?" These are questions that anyone who has carried out a responsibility, whether volunteer or paid, has probably asked.

The volunteer leader has the right to know the answers to these questions. If it was a good job, volunteer leaders may wonder, "What did I do that made it good? What were the strengths and weaknesses in my accomplishments? How can I do better next time I'm asked to assume a responsibility? But was it really good—or are people just being proper and polite? Is it a 'tongue-in-cheek' bit of feedback?"

In the involvement of volunteer leadership in the church we have too long ignored evaluation. The results are often noticeable:

- ingrown leadership,
- ineffective leadership,
- inadequacy of the mission and ministry to which we have made a commitment, personally and corporately.

Those who work with volunteers have the responsibility for providing a time of evaluation with each volunteer.

"Evaluation is the act of comparing what is done with what is supposed to be accomplished. It is a time when deeds are measured against goals. In most instances, people consider evaluation to be a trying time, no matter when or where it is done. However, if evaluation is done correctly, it can be a means of support, training, and redirection. The evaluation process and end results are key factors. Using a few principles of evaluation in the church helps people to grow and the total program to become more effective."[9]

Some basic principles for evaluation may serve as guidelines.

1. Begin with informal conversation where both parties involved can talk about the fulfillment and frustrations in the caring for the responsibility. This is a feeling-level conversation and may provide information to be pursued later on in the evaluation.

2. Make evaluation a time of affirmation and celebration.

3. Base the evaluation on the goals, personal and corporate, identified at the start of the volunteer leader's responsibility.[10] The end result of the evaluation should be:

- a clear understanding of the particular strengths and weaknesses that the volunteer has demonstrated in the specific responsibility;
- the setting of new, revised, or reaffirmed goals for the volunteer leader;
- an indication of where and how the volunteer leader would like to be included in future leadership in or through the congregation.

Some persons would say that evaluation reflects too much of the business or professional world. The assumption behind evaluation is that the ministry of Jesus Christ, as enacted by the congregation, deserves nothing but the best that can be offered. Jesus required such of the disciples. He held them mutually responsible (see Mark 10:42-45). We who follow as today's disciples can do no less than to hold each other responsible as disciples.

---

[9] Douglas Johnson, *Empowering Lay Volunteers* (Nashville: Abingdon Press, 1991), 105.
[10] *Ibid.*, 105, adapted.

We are not suggesting a hierarchial system of accountability. Evaluation in terms of volunteer leadership in the church is a matter of mutuality. In a one-with-one evaluation experience two disciples are pausing to ask, "How are we doing in carrying out the ministry that Jesus has called us to?"

That is the essence of evaluation.

In Conclusion

The following brings our exploration of voluntary leadership into perspective:
"What volunteers repeatedly have said they want and need are:
- to be carefully interviewed and appropriately assigned to a meaningful task;
- to receive training and supervision to help them to do that task well;
- to be involved in planning and evaluating the program in which they participate;
- to receive recognition in a way that is meaningful to them;
- to be regarded as persons of uniqueness;
- to be accepted as a valued member of the team."[11]

---

[11] Marlene Wilson, *How to Mobilize Church Volunteers* (Minneapolis: Augsburg, 1983), 47.

Chapter 12

Planning for Effective and Vital Christian Education

The primary task of the group responsible for Christian education is to plan and implement the total educational ministry of the local church. How this is done is a significant consideration for the board, committee, or group responsible.

Appendix A, Evaluation Form, is organized around nine characteristics of effective and vital Christian education. It, along with the planning process described in this chapter, is planned to help a board, committee, or group evaluate its present educational program and plan for its future educational ministry and programs.

The nine characteristics of effective and vital Christian education grow out of Search Institute's study of effective Christian education in six major protestant denominations.[1] Completed in 1990, the study concluded that the congregational factor most associated with helping people grow in faith maturity is the degree of effectiveness in Christian education programming. How then can we describe effective—and vital—Christian education?

Let's begin that description with nine characteristics:

1. The church gives priority to Christian education and understands that it is more than just Sunday church school.

2. The pastor is committed, involved, and trained in relation to Christian education.

3. Teachers and leaders are knowledgeable, committed, caring, and teachable.

4. The teaching ministry with adults is given a strong emphasis and programs for children and youth are offered.

5. The content offered for study addresses biblical understanding, global awareness, moral and value issues, and social issues.

6. A variety of learning activities are used for all age levels.

---

[1] For more information about this study write Search Institute, 122 West Franklin Ave., Minneapolis, MN 55404 or call 612/870-9511.

7. Strong administrative foundations are in place.
8. Parents and guardians are supported in their "teaching" roles.
9. Members are informed, eager, and enthusiastic about the teaching ministry.

The Evaluation Form

The Evaluation Form (Appendix A) is organized around the nine characteristics of effective and vital Christian education. Each characteristic is listed with several "indicators of evidence" of that characteristic and there is room for the evaluator(s) to add more indicators for each characteristic. Persons completing the form are asked to rank their church's Christian education by putting the appropriate numeral on the blank to the left of each statement:

1 = strong
2 = adequate
3 = needs improvement.

After ranking all indicators each person is asked to review his or her work and star(*) one or two (not more than three per sheet!) that they feel deserve priority attention by their church. Your starred items may include items ranked #1, 2, or 3. The right-hand column provides room to make notes about next steps.

The form is designed for use with a variety of persons within the congregation. Apart from its function of evaluation, a primary purpose of the form is consciousness-raising. The form suggests both to those who complete it and to the planners who use it what the essential elements are in an effective and vital total educational program in a church. In other words, the use of the form can be an educational experience, helping persons to develop a vision of the "ideal" or a dream of "what can be." The use of the form, along with reflection on the results, can be a challenge to planners as they define and seek effectiveness and vitality in their program of Christian education.

It is possible that at first glance the "ideal" situation, set forth by the statements on the Evaluation Form, may seem like a heavy burden for the board of Christian education. It is important for the board to realize that, while the form is intended to suggest a wide variety of possibilities, no church is the "ideal." Each board has to determine the areas most needing attention in its own church and to plan to strengthen those areas. Sometimes that means enhancing a strength! The evaluation-form responses, when analyzed, can be helpful in determining the educational needs of the church.

Furthermore, the board of Christian education may wish to explore with other boards and groups their relationship to certain areas or needs suggested by the evaluations.

A Suggested Planning Process

It will take several hours in a retreat setting or several evening meetings for the board to use the first six steps in this suggested planning process. The process also involves as many members of the congregation as possible. If several sessions are planned, it is most desirable that in the first session the board complete step I. Note that step II needs to be completed before the session in which step III is done. Plan to cover steps III and IV in session two (note that step IV suggests the involvement of other people in the congregation and therefore requires some preplanning), step V in session three, and step VI in session four. If the process is done in a retreat setting, preplanning will be needed in order to have evaluation-form responses for step II, and follow-up work for step IV will be needed in order to build ownership within the congregation. Steps VII and VIII are essential to the process but occur after the retreat or four planning sessions. Be sure to read through the entire process and then decide how best to proceed for your situation.

The steps in the planning process are:

Step I: Review the concept of a teaching church, the goal of the church's teaching ministry, and the nine characteristics of effective Christian education.

In chapter 1 of this manual there are three affirmations about a teaching church and a statement of the five basic functions of a teaching church. The goal of the church's teaching ministry can be found in chapter 2 and the nine characteristics are mentioned earlier in this chapter and in Appendix A. Time should be provided for the board to read and discuss this material. This material may be duplicated for use with the group.

Step II: Evaluate the church's Christian education in relation to the nine characteristics.

1. Have each member of the board individually complete an evaluation form (Appendix A).

2. Have a wide range of persons complete the Evaluation Form.

Include members of classes and groups (church school classes, women's groups, and so forth), designated leaders (members of boards, committees, and officers), and other persons (such as those in attendance in a worship service). Request time during classes, group meetings, and worship services for persons to complete forms. The forms should be completed on an individual basis, even though group time may be used.

Step III: Collate and analyze the Evaluation Form responses.

1. Collate the responses item by item on a blank response sheet.

2. When all the forms have been collated begin the analysis. Look for common responses among the starred (*) items first, then among the items rated 1 (strengths), 2 (adequate), and 3 (needs improvement), noting trends. Then note significant differences of opinion that seem to be present. It is important to collate the responses separately by groups (for example, the board of Christian education, teachers, adult students, and so forth) so a comparison of results can be made. A study and comparison of the responses will give a picture of the apparent strengths and weaknesses of Christian education in the congregation. You may wish to have the collation done prior to the planning session in which it will be considered.

3. Review current Christian education programs. Make a list of all current Christian education programs, activities, and events in order to have a more complete picture of Christian education in the congregation. Organize these under the categories of the nine characteristics of effective and vital Christian education. It may be helpful to include in your list policies and procedures as well. Remember that just because you are doing these things now does not mean that they should continue forever. One test of their effectiveness is to see to what extent they were mentioned by persons completing the Evaluation Form.

Step IV: Determine the areas most needing improvement or attention.

1. Compile this list from those starred (*) in the evaluation form responses. Divide the list into three parts to show:

   a. Needs we should work on now (immediately),

   b. Needs we should work on in the near future (soon),

   c. Needs we should work on when we can (long-range).

You may want to code these to further distinguish them; for example: a = green, b = yellow, c = blue. Do not try to work on all of the needs at one time. Some should be done first because the need is greatest or because they are key to getting others done. Narrow the top priorities down to no more than three, ranking them 1, 2, and 3.

2. Share the prioritized list with everyone who completed an Evaluation Form. Such involvement can help develop ownership in the wider congregation.

Step V: Write objectives for the year.

1. Determine from your prioritized list of needs those that will be worked on during the coming year.

2. State these needs as objectives. Relate them to the overall goal of Christian education, the five functions of a teaching church, and the nine characteristics of effective and vital Christian education.

Objectives are statements of hoped-for outcome. They are specific, achievable within a stated period of time, measurable, and stated in terms of the audience to be served. In other words, an objective states **who** is to be involved or helped, **what** is to be done, and **by when** this is to happen.

Here are some sample objectives:

- To involve 50 percent of our parents of young children in Bible study this fall.
- To have potential leaders of adult classes and groups complete a training course by February 15.
- To involve church officers in a planning retreat in April for study and consciousness raising regarding how the whole church teaches and learns in both planned and unplanned ways.

Note how each objective answers three questions: Who? What? By when?

Step VI: Write an action plan for each objective.

Develop an action plan for each objective. An action plan is the stated plan of action for accomplishing the objective. Each action plan needs to include the following:

- the statement of objective,
- a brief description of the program, event, activity, or task anticipated,
- the person(s) who is to be invited to implement the plan on behalf of the board,
- the completion date.

Step VII: Implement the action plans.

Invite, work with, and support the persons implementing the action plans. Plan periodic reports to the board or committee responsible.

Step VIII: Evaluate the growth in effective and vital Christian education throughout the year.

Do this much as you check the oil level in your car's engine using a dip stick. Take quick checks periodically. Ask how it is going, how we are doing, and to what extent we are accomplishing what we set out to do.

Evaluate after each program with leaders and as a board or committee of Christian education. Evaluate annually the effectiveness of objectives, action plans, and implementation of plans with the board or committee of Christian education in preparation for planning for the next year. Involve as many members of the congregation as possible. Include children, youth, and adults—visitors, too, from time to time.

Chapter 13

Congregational Support

An effective teaching ministry is an all-church task, not just the special concern of a few "dedicated" members who serve on the board or teach in the church school or work with the youth.

It's Our Work (or "They" Is Us)

The whole church teaches. Everything in the life and work of a congregation has educational effects—good or bad. A congregation affirms educational ministry in some very concrete ways, such as providing financial support for programs and resources. Congregational awareness of and participation in the educational program and goals is another vital aspect of support. Without congregational support, the church's educational ministry becomes a "special interest" project dependent on the commitment of certain persons who "believe in Christian education." In such cases, what the church teaches is that Christian education is important for a few people but not for the church as a whole.

Congregational support can be developed. It grows when a congregation (1) feels included in planning and decision making, (2) has information, and (3) is held accountable.

Include the Congregation

The board has some responsibility for helping the congregation to have a sense of ownership in the educational program. Congregational apathy and indifference are frequently the result of not feeling included in planning, envisioning, and decision making related to the teaching ministry. The congregation is a part of the educational team. The quality of the teamwork will determine how effectively a church works at the goal of helping persons to commit their lives to Christ and grow in Christian discipleship.

The healthy functioning of the church—the body of Christ—depends on the various parts of the body working together. (See Ephesians 4.)

Seeking input on what programs are needed and providing programs that meet needs are additional ways to include the congregation. Involvement as a participant may also lead to persons becoming leaders.

Helping the congregation catch a vision, see the possibilities, or understand the goals of a congregation's educational program can be done in some limited ways through worship. Planning a worship service or regular services that focus on the value and place of education is a good way to reach a significant portion of the congregation. Using appropriate litanies and hymns involves people directly with important ideas and key concepts.

Provide Information

Providing information is basic in helping the congregation to feel a part of the educational team.

Members of a church need information about their educational goals and program—current and potential. The board of Christian education can take responsibility for providing information through regular reporting, letters, announcements, or visual presentations in congregational meetings, items in bulletins and newsletters, posters, and exhibits.

The congregation needs to know who the designated leaders are—board members, teachers, youth leaders, and others. They need to be kept informed throughout the year about current happenings, concerns, achievements, and planning—both short-term and long-range.

Expect Accountability

The shared expectations and reporting of a board of Christian education can help a congregation acknowledge its responsibility and give appropriate support. Clear reports about accomplishments and needs and unapologetic requests for funds and leaders help a congregation to participate in the "whole church program" of education. Careful planning and reporting help the church to grow in a caring awareness that its educational ministry is not something "they" (a few dedicated members) do, but something very significant that WE DO TOGETHER. "But speaking the truth in love, we must grow up in every way into him who is the head, into Christ, from whom the whole body, joined and knit together by every ligament with which it is equipped, as each part is working properly, promotes the body's growth in building itself up in love" (Ephesians 4:15-16).

Evaluation Form

Planning for Effective and Vital Christian Education

1. Rate your congregation's Christian education by putting the appropriate numeral on the blank to the left of each statement:

    1 = strong
    2 = adequate
    3 = needs improvement

    Note that there is space to add additional descriptive statements for each characteristic.

2. Review your ratings and from among all nine character indices, star (*) the one or two (not more than 3!) needing attention first.

3. In the right hand column, "Concerns/Next Steps," jot down concerns you have or steps you think could be taken.

Characteristics of Effective and Vital Christian Education	**Concerns/Next Steps**

1. The church gives priority to Christian education (CE) and understands that it is more than just Sunday church school.

____ adequate financial support given

____ frequent mention of CE in public places (bulletin, bulletin board, newsletter, etc.)

____ adequate time set aside for formal CE

____ informal teaching and learning recognized and affirmed

____ Christian education takes place in a variety of settings (committees, choirs, worship, special events, etc.)

____

____

2. The pastor is committed to, involved in, and trained in Christian education.

____ teaches a class or group

____ attends CE board meetings

____ openly advocates for CE

____ preaches "teaching" sermons

____ supports teachers and leaders

____

____

3. Teachers and leaders are knowledgeable, committed, caring, and teachable.

____ attend training events

____ tend to their own spiritual growth

____ spend time outside class with those they teach

____ are themselves open to learning and growing

____ know the Bible and teaching methods

____ keep abreast of current information and skills related to their responsibilities, whether teacher, group leader, committee chair, church officer, and so forth.

____

____

4. The teaching ministry with adults is given a strong emphasis.

____ choices of study offered

____ in-depth Bible study available

____ small groups provided

____ in auxiliary groups, boards (deacons, trustees, etc.), committees, choirs

____

____

Characteristics of Effective and Vital Christian Education

Concerns/Next Steps

5. Programs for children are offered.

_____ during Sunday church school

_____ during the week, after school or evening

_____ weekday nursery school and/or child care

_____ camping opportunities for elementary age children

_____ community outreach ministries

_____ choirs or musical groups

_____

_____

6. Programs for youth are offered.

_____ classes during Sunday church school

_____ evening fellowship group(s)

_____ camp and conference opportunities

_____ choirs or musical groups

_____ community outreach ministries

_____ college, career, and/or job counseling

_____

_____

_____

7. The content offered for study addresses:

_____ biblical understanding

_____ global awareness

_____ moral and value issues

_____ social issues

_____

_____

8. A variety of learning activities is used for all age levels.

_____ A-V equipment available

_____ resource center available

_____ teachers use stories, visuals, activities, etc.

_____ teachers encouraged to use a variety of methods and to try new methods

_____ mission tours, work groups, and service projects included as learning activities

_____

_____

Characteristics of Effective and Vital Christian Education

9. Strong administrative foundations are in place.

_____ teacher/leader recruitment

_____ teacher/leader recognition

_____ teacher/leader training

_____ teacher/leader support

_____ teacher/leader faith formation (spiritual growth)

_____ program goals and objectives stated and known

_____ evaluation done regularly

_____ governing body support strong

_____

_____

10. Parents and guardians are supported in their "teaching" roles.

_____ Family worship ideas (including special seasons such as Advent, Lent) provided

_____ parenting classes offered

_____ Bible study groups for parents offered

_____ family life center provided

_____

_____

11. Members are informed, eager, and enthusiastic about the teaching ministry.

_____ tell newcomers about programs

_____ invite new people to attend

_____ offer to help carry out the teaching ministry

_____

_____

Resources for the Board of Christian Education

General Administration

Chism, Keith A. *Christian Education for the African American Community*. Nashville: Discipleship Resources, 1996.

Griggs, Donald L., and Walther, Judy M. *Christian Education in the Small Church*. Valley Forge: Judson Press, 1988.

Hanson, Grant W. *Foundations for the Teaching Church*. Valley Forge: Judson Press, 1986.

Isham, Linda R. *Charting Our Course: Renewing the Church's Teaching Ministry*. Valley Forge: Judson Press, 1997.

Jones, Idris W., revised by Ruth L. Spencer. *The Work of the Sunday School Superintendent, Revised Edition*. Valley Forge: Judson Press, 1994.

Massey, Floyd, Jr., and McKinney, Samuel B. *Church Administration: The Black Perspective*. Valley Forge: Judson Press, 1976.

Sawyer, David R. *Work of the Church: Getting the Job Done in Boards and Committees*. Valley Forge: Judson Press, 1987.

Seymour, Jack, ed. *Mapping Christian Education: Fresh Approaches to Congregations*. Nashville: Abingdon Press, 1997.

Leader Development

Burt, Steve. *Activating Leadership in the Small Church: Clergy and Laity Working Together*. Valley Forge: Judson Press, 1988.

Callahan, Kennon L. *Effective Church Leadership: Building on the Twelve Keys*. San Francisco: Harper, 1990. Second edition available from Jossey-Bass.

Chartier, Jan. *Desarollo del Liderazgo en la Iglesia que Educa*. Valley Forge: Judson Press, 1992.

Greenleaf, Robert K. *Servant Leadership: A Journey into the Nature of Legitimate Power and Greatness.* New York: Paulist Press, 1977.

Morris, Margie. *Volunteer Ministries: New Strategies for Today's Church.* Sherman, Texas: Newton-Cline Press, 1991.

Morris, Margie, and Stephens, Jessie Gunn. *Volunteer Management: Workshop Leader's Guide.* Sherman, Texas: Newton-Cline Press, 1991.

Ratcliff, Donald, and Neff, Blake. *The Complete Guide to Religious Education Volunteers.* Birmingham: Religious Education Press, 1992.

Rusbuldt, Richard E. *Basic Leader Skills: Handbook for Church Leaders.* Valley Forge: Judson Press, 1981.

Rusbuldt, Richard E. *Basic Teacher Skills: Handbook for Church School Teachers, Revised Edition.* Valley Forge: Judson Press, 1997.

Turner, Nathan W. *Leading Small Groups: Basic Skills for Church and Community Organizations.* Valley Forge: Judson Press, 1996.

Wilson, Marlene. *How to Mobilize Church Volunteers.* Minneapolis: Augsburg Fortress Press, 1983.

Children's Ministry

Bruce, Barbara. *7 Ways of Teaching the Bible to Children.* Nashville: Abingdon Press, 1996.

Carlson, Lee W. *Child Sexual Abuse: A Handbook for Clergy and Church Members.* Valley Forge: Judson Press, 1988.

Hale-Benson, Janice E. *Black Children: Their Roots, Culture, and Learning Styles,* rev. ed. Baltimore: Johns Hopkins University Press, 1986.

Heusser, D-B and Heusser, Phyllis. *Children as Partners in the Church.* Valley Forge: Judson Press, 1985.

Johnson, Evelyn M., and Bower, Bobbie. *Building a Great Children's Ministry.* Nashville: Abingdon Press, 1992.

Ng, David, and Thomas, Virginia. *Children in the Worshipping Community.* Louisville: Westminster/John Knox Press, 1981.

O'Neal, Debbie Trafton. *More than Glue and Glitter.* Minneapolis: Augsburg Fortress, 1992.

Youth Ministry

Brown, Carolyn. *Youth Ministries: Thinking Big with Small Groups.* Nashville: Abingdon Press, 1984.

Foster. Charles R., and Shockley, Grant S., eds. *Working with Black Youth: Opportunities for Christian Ministry.* Nashville: Abingdon Press, 1989.

Jones, Jeffrey D., and Potts, Kenneth C. *Organizing a Youth Ministry to Fit Your Needs.* Valley Forge: Judson Press, 1983.

Jones, Stephen D. *Faith Shaping: Youth and the Experience of Faith,* rev. ed. Valley Forge: Judson Press, 1987.

Adult Ministry

Myers, William, *Black and White Styles of Youth Ministry: Two Congregations in America.* Cleveland: Pilgrim Press, 1990.

Ng, David. *Developing Leaders for Youth Ministry.* Valley Forge: Judson Press, 1984.

Vázquez, Victor, M, ed. *La Juventud: Discipulado para Hoy.* Valley Forge: Judson Press, 1989.

Adult Ministry

Brookfield, Stephen J. *Understanding and Facilitating Adult Learning: A Comprehensive Analysis of Principles and Effective Practices.* San Francisco: Jossey-Bass, 1991.

Foltz,· Nancy T. *Handbook of Adult Religious Education.* Birmingham: Religious Education Press, 1986.

Gribbon, Robert T. *Developing Faith in Young Adults: Effective Ministry with 18-35 Year Olds.* Washington, D.C.: Alban Institute, 1990.

Osmer, Robert. *Teaching for Faith: A Guide for Teachers of Adult Classes.* Louisville: Westminister/John Knox Press, 1992.

Vogel, Linda J. *The Religious Education of Older Adults.* Birmingham: Religious Education Press, 1984.

Church School

Griggs, Donald L., *Planning for Teaching Church School.* Valley Forge: Judson Press, 1985.

Jones, Idris W., revised by Ruth L. Spencer. *The Work of the Sunday School Superintendent, Revised Edition.* Valley Forge: Judson Press, 1994.

Family Ministry

Adams, Doug, ed. *Children, Divorce and the Church.* Nashville: Abingdon Press, 1993.

Allen, Karen L., and Allen, Gary G. *Roots and Wings: Discovering and Developing Family Strengths.* Cleveland: Pilgrim Press, 1992.

Bernstine, Karen Jones, ed. *Church and Family Together: A Congregational Manual for Black Family Ministry.* Valley Forge: Judson Press, 1996.

Friedman, Edwin H. *Generation to Generation: Family Process in Church and Synagogue.* New York: Guilford Press, 1986.

Smith, Wallace C. *The Church in the Life of the Black Family.* Valley Forge: Judson Press, 1985.

Mission Education

Bauer, Arthur. *Being in Mission: A Resource for th Local Church and Community* (Making Mission Happen). New York: Friendship Press, 1987.